# Saving Belief

Centre for
Faith and Spirituality
Loughborough University

*Library of Anglican Spirituality*

# SAVING BELIEF

*A Discussion of Essentials*

## AUSTIN FARRER

MOWBRAY

MOREHOUSE PUBLISHING

**Mowbray**
A Cassell imprint
Villiers House
41/47 Strand
London
WC2N 5JE

**Morehouse Publishing**
P.O. Box 1321
Harrisburg, PA 17105

First published 1964 by Hodder and Stoughton
First published in this series 1994

British Library Cataloguing-in-Publication Data
A catalogue entry for this book is available from the British Library.
Library of Congress Cataloging-in-Publication Data
A catalog entry for this book is available from the Library of Congress.

ISBN 0-264-67257-3 (Mowbray)
0-8192-1625-9 (Morehouse)

Printed and bound in Great Britain by
Mackays of Chatham PLC

# Series Foreword

THIS series is designed for the intelligent reader with a good grasp of reality and a generous amount of common sense who wants to know more about ultimate reality and the profoundest truths of human existence. Any religion worthy of the name is concerned with questions of meaning and value. Christianity is one of the great religions of the world and for nearly two thousand years has been subjected to the closest scrutiny by some of the finest intellects which have ever existed. The purpose of this series is to share some of the wisdom of the leading lights of the Church of England in the twentieth century who have written of the ceaseless human quest to make sense of the world — and so attain the richest possible life — the Life which we all yearn to have in abundance but which too frequently eludes our uncertain grasp.

I first became interested in the great Anglican writers of modern times when I was researching my six novels about the Church of England in the twentieth century. The research involved not only studying Church history but familiarizing myself with the writings, theological and occasionally auto-biographical, of prominent modern churchmen. In the end I found a number of churchmen so fascinating and their writings so riveting that I quoted from their books regularly in my novels.

Unfortunately much theology dates, but I discovered there are two types of work which survive the passing decades: first-class explorations of the psyche (since the best writing on mysticism and spirituality is timeless) and first-class expositions of classic Christian doctrine (since the truths being presented are eternal). In the first four books in the Library of Anglican Spirituality, Reginald Somerset Ward and Harry Williams explore the psyche while Austin Farrer and Dorothy L. Sayers expound doctrine, but inevitably there is overlapping as apologetic shades into spirituality and spirituality illuminates apologetic. All represent the Church of England in either a traditional or a liberal form, and the next four books in the series will continue to explore these two complementary facets of modern Anglicanism.

It remains only for me to commend these authors, who have given me so much enlightenment, and to thank Mowbray for their decision to make these stimulating masterpieces available to the modern reader.

Susan Howatch

# Introduction

'CAN reasonable minds still think theologically?' asks Austin Farrer with brutal frankness in the Preface of *Saving Belief*. The rest of the book is spent triumphantly answering his question in the affirmative. Here is one of the great theological intellects of the twentieth century demonstrating his genius with a light touch and readable skill.

Farrer was born in 1904. Educated at St. Paul's School in London, he won a scholarship to Balliol College, Oxford, where he obtained a first in Mods and Greats (Classical Moderations and Literae Humaniores) and a first in theology; he was awarded a doctorate in divinity in 1945. His parents were Baptists, but during his time up at Oxford he became a member of the Church of England, and having decided to train for the priesthood he was ordained deacon in 1928. He then spent time in a Yorkshire parish not far from Leeds before returning to Oxford as chaplain and tutor at St. Edmund Hall. Soon afterwards his friendship began with Katharine Newton who in 1937 was to become his wife; she was an undergraduate, and when she had taken her degree they became secretly engaged. In 1935 he moved from St. Edmund Hall to become Chaplain of Trinity College. His work here used his gifts to the full, but eventually he felt the time had come to move on, and after failing to be appointed Regius Professor of Divinity he became Warden of Keble in 1960.

During his twenty-five years at Trinity Farrer taught both philosophy and theology. Moreover, he lectured not only on the philosophy of the past but on the philosophy of modern times and was well acquainted with those systems hostile to religion. He became famous as the result of his Bampton Lectures (published as *The Glass of Vision* in 1948) and during his last years he wrote a succession of acclaimed works including *Faith and Speculation, Love Almighty and Ills Unlimited* and this present book. Several volumes of his sermons were published both before and after his death in 1968. These sermons were highly regarded; they would usually begin with an incident recalled from everyday life and end with an unabashed lauding of the triune God. Conversational yet literary, effortlessly delivered yet intricately constructed, they provide a seamless, panoramic vista of his theology, his philosophy and his life in mid-century Oxford.

*Saving Belief* does not consist of sermons, but the text was based on a set of lectures given to undergraduates; so the style is not dissimilar: Farrer chats away with deceptive simplicity about the most profound and complex facets of the Christian faith. What sort of Christian was Farrer? He can be described as a Prayer-Book Anglican in the Tractarian tradition — one might say he was a quintessential Anglican Catholic, although he believed that Protestant and Catholic doctrine were not fundamentally opposed and that each needed the other. He was classically orthodox, a theologian utterly committed to the doctrine of the Trinity and supremely adept at expounding it. Yet this emphasis on his theological orthodoxy is misleading because it suggests someone addicted to 'playing safe' and Farrer was adventurous. From the secure base provided by his orthodoxy he was constantly speculating, constantly engaging in dialogue with those who did not think as he did, constantly engaging in dialogue too with himself as he worked out his philosophical and theological stances. Grappling with Bultmann's liberalism, standing fast amidst the radical explosions of the 1960s, jousting with the heavyweights of biblical scholarship, looking clear-eyed into the reductionist abyss created by the logical positivists, Farrer was fearless. He flinched from nothing. He faced everything. Yet there was nothing bombastic about him. As C. S. Lewis said, Farrer remained patient and modest, but the sheer costliness of this intellectual bravery must have been considerable, particularly when he also had to cope with a difficult home life; his wife became addicted to alcohol and his only child, a daughter, had learning difficulties. One would like to know, perhaps, why Mrs. Farrer became addicted to alcohol, but one can only admire Farrer's heroism in looking after her in trying circumstances. It was not altogether surprising that he eventually died, aged only sixty-four, after months of strain and overwork.

When considering Farrer's life it is hard to resist the conclusion that he was born out of his time. Intellectually he would have been more at home with the medieval Scholastics, devoted as they were to reason and logic and to the inheritance of Aristotle which St. Thomas Aquinas was to explore so fruitfully. Alternatively, one can visualize him being at ease a hundred and fifty years ago with the leaders of the Oxford Movement, who were so dedicated to reviving the Catholic tradition within the Church of England and underpinning that revival with scholarly writing. It is startling to remember, as one reads Farrer's sermons, that he was preaching them at Oxford while Harry Williams was delivering his radically innovative sermons at Cambridge — and perhaps it is even more startling to reflect that this present book was published a year after John Robinson's *Honest to God*.

*Saving Belief* is Farrer's one systematic treatise on theology and provides a brief but luminous statement of his Trinitarian belief and Catholic faith. The book is important for today simply because it is so orthodox: here is a gifted theologian passing on the classical form of a timeless tradition with great force and skill. In an age of easy relativism where every belief, no matter how mindless, is thought by some to be as valid as any other, it is also salutary to be reminded of Christianity's powerful intellectual dimension. For two thousand years the best minds have been writing about the Christian faith; Farrer encapsulates this accumulated wisdom, and by doing so reminds us that far too many people today dismiss Christianity without ever taking the trouble to discover how intellectually satisfying it is. Indeed it may be thought that one of the strongest arguments in favour of Christianity lies in considering the vast range of brilliant thinkers who have found it credible.

In addition one can argue that it is only after receiving a grounding in orthodox doctrine that one can fairly judge the efforts of today's liberal-radicals who are trying to restate the tradition. How can one either approve or condemn this updating of the Christian message unless one understands exactly what is being updated? This book is subtitled 'A Discussion of Essentials'. Essentials indeed they are, as essential for us in the pessimistic 1990s as they were for the undergraduates who listened to Farrer's words amidst the heady optimism which marked the Swinging Sixties.

Nevertheless, thirty years have passed since this book was first published and it is important not to react too fiercely to the few passages which jolt the modern eye. It will be noticed, for example, that Farrer often seems oblivious of the fact that the human race consists of women as well as men. Similarly he is unfashionably robust in his dismissal of world religions other than Christianity. In our Orwellian age, where we suffer increasingly from the tyranny of political correctness, it would be easy to criticize Farrer in these instances, but to judge the members of a previous generation in the light of the social attitudes and conventions of our time would be unfair. Farrer was a man of great integrity who was interested not in ephemeral fashion but in eternal truth. In our increasingly fragmented and disorientated world we have much to learn from him.

'We must put our confidence in *truth*', wrote Farrer. 'But that doesn't mean sitting back, and waiting for the truth to shine from above, as one might sit back and wait for the day to break. It means following with devoted obedience the truth *we have seen* as true, with an entire confidence in God, that he will correct, clear and redirect our vision, to the perception of a freer and deeper truth.' His many loyal followers alive today would claim these were the words of a religious genius, even of a saint. They are certainly the words of a brilliant Christian scholar, and Austin Farrer deserves to be read today by all those interested in truth, tradition and twentieth-century spirituality.

Susan Howatch

# Preface

CAN reasonable minds still think theologically? How much, if so, of the traditional pattern must they discard? Is theology a science, or can it be made so? And if not, what then? These are questions widely canvassed at the present time; and it is tempting to suppose that we cannot usefully do any theology until we have settled them. I strongly suspect that the very reverse is the truth. Here am I shivering on the brink of the pool. Do I remember the strokes? Can I bear the temperature? If I get a mouthful and choke, what do I do? Pressing questions, these. I shall know the answers if I jump in. Can theology be done, and if so, how? Plunge into it, and see; how else are you ever to find out? Think your way through your faith, and the answers to your enquiries will keep tumbling in: how it fits with the rest of your mental furniture, how traditionally or non-traditionally styled it is, and (of course) whether you believe it.

These happy discoveries will come to hand if we do our religious thinking like honest men, and in one piece with our thinking on other subjects. The temptation is no doubt strong to slip away into a museum of medieval or scriptural images, and to work out a pious pattern unrelated to the way we think about anything else. Whether I have fallen into this foible I can only ask my readers to judge. My intention is to offer them a very slight and incomplete exercise in thinking through. It was performed for a non-specialist audience of undergraduates, but they too are men and I hope it may prove of wider interest. The field of discussion is limited to saving faith and the objects of its belief. I trust that I have gone to the heart of the matter. I know I have not achieved systematic completeness nor attempted topical application. There is nothing in these pages about nuclear bombs, artificial insemination, free love, world government, Church reunion, or the restyling of public worship. Those who seek after news may save their pains.

Oxford.

*Easter*, 1963.

# Contents

# Faith and Evidence

Approaching the Christian religion from without, and wondering how people get in, one meets the strange assertion that the key of entry is faith. Those who have faith (it seems) can turn the lock; those who have none stay outside. The assertion sounds baffling to would-be entrants, and fishy to detached critics. A great deal has been said and a great deal written by the keepers of the door, to explain how keys can be cut, and how the lock can be lubricated; but it never seems quite good enough, and so we find ourselves trying again.

What are we to say? First of all, that faith is not any sort of instrument, or tackle, with which we can arm ourselves beforehand; nothing like a key or, to change the figure, nothing like a fishing-line with which religious convictions are hooked and drawn to land. We must provide ourselves with tackle before we can usefully think of fishing a pond; but faith is not a tackle, but (shall we say?) an attitude of mind, and it is an awkward job to take up an attitude, until you are face to face with the object which calls for it. When we want to make fun of the more portentous Germans, we say they are the sort to take up attitudes of welcome or of distrust, of mastery or of reverence, towards existence, or towards things in general, without first considering whether the objects they encounter are such as to call for the attitudes they adopt. The accusation is probably as unjust as other generalizations about national characteristics; we are less

I

concerned to accuse the Germans than we are to flatter ourselves. We, of course, are men who appreciate our objects, and let our objects determine our attitudes. We think it silly to treat animals (for example) as if they were persons, and imperceptive to treat them as though they were machines. Only if we appreciate them for what they are, shall we react to them as they deserve. Is religious faith the appropriate attitude to deity? If it is, we cannot talk much sense about it, until we first have some perception, or conception, of God.

It does not look as though we should get faith first, and the object of faith second; nor do we in fact. What does happen to us, and how is it that we get round to raising the issue of faith? It begins with our hearing about God or, if we are clever enough, thinking thoughts about him for ourselves. If anything of importance is to follow, the thought we think, or the tale we are told, must be initially persuasive. We must feel, as we say, the force of it. At least part of our mind must be saying, Yes, surely there *is* a first creative cause, surely there *is* a supreme directive will, a saviour of men, a bestower of grace, or whatever it be. But presently, being reasonable people, we ask ourselves what is the basis of our feeling or persuasion that such things are at all true. In answer to our own question we may state plenty of reasons for believing such things. In spite of all the subtleties of the philosophers, I still think there must be some exterior cause or maker of the world; or I tell myself that the virtue of the heroic saints is something which irreligion does not produce, and which goes above human nature; and I am not prepared to brush aside these men's own account of what it is that has happened to them. Here are reasons, reasons of a kind; and for a while we may be highly pleased with them. But it will not be long before we become aware of opposing reasons; and there seems to be no simple logical method for deciding conclusively between the *pros* and the *cons*. No simple logical method, no, nor any advanced logical method, either. For only look at those famous philosophical twins, Russell and Whitehead, the co-inventors of mathematical logic and the joint authors of an epoch-making book. One of them turned out an atheist, the other a theist; and neither could show the other the error of his ways. Russell now has the advantage, in the continued opportunity to propagate his ideas; but Whitehead has the advantage (let us hope) of now knowing conclusively that Russell is wrong.

Met by such facts as these, we are driven to ask what it is that decides our minds for, or against, religious conviction. Since it is not sheer logic, or plain evidence, what can it be? What but the faith which one man has, and another has not? The believer gives his confidence to the positive reasons, as a voter gives his confidence to the Liberals. The voter knows perfectly well that the practicability or the usefulness of the Liberal proposals can be plausibly contested; but still, on balance, he decides to support them. He has a faith in Liberalism. And so, we may suppose, a man has faith in God.

There is some merit in the political comparison; it brings out the practical character of the decision. If we say to the ardent politician, 'Why not leave the issue open? After all, you can't be sure,' we know very well what he will reply. 'The country's going to the dogs; we can't sit with our hands in our laps. If we do nothing, we are for it, anyway. It may be there are better remedies than those we propose, but meanwhile things

3

are going from bad to worse and we can't wait ever-lastingly for Royal Commissions to send in reports.' And so a believer may say, 'I've only seventy years, if that, to make anything of my life; I can't indefinitely postpone the question whether I have a God or whether I have to be God to myself.'

But we must not exaggerate the role of practical urgency. It justifies acting upon faith; it does not make the faith. If a man says, 'It's urgent that something should be done and I've a vote; so I'll spin a coin between the Liberals and the Socialists,' then even if the penny comes down on the Liberal side of the argument, the voter cannot be said to have faith in Liberalism. Faith implies genuine persuasion; and persuasion is not genuine unless it comes from the thing which persuades us. It cannot be got going by stoking up the furnaces of the will.

The believer in Liberalism, like the believer in God, is first captured by a story. It is only afterwards that he becomes aware of the faith-factor in his being so captured; and that happens when he becomes aware of counter-persuasions, yet persists in his Liberal conviction. The counter-persuasions make him aware of the faith-factor; they do not create it. Faith becomes self-conscious in exerting itself against the counter-persuasions; but it was there already. It was, in fact, built into the persuasion from the start. Liberalism is, as we say, a political faith.

We see, then, that faith is neither an attitude we adopt in looking for an object of conviction, nor an attitude we work up to bolster a conviction already lodged in our minds. Either we are persuaded or not persuaded, that is the starting-point. If we are persuaded, some element of

4

faith is there; it is a matter of its maintaining itself or not maintaining itself against rival persuasions.

The difficulty about faith is not a difficulty about faith in general, or about the enormous part that it plays in every department of life. The difficulty about faith is a difficulty about religious faith in particular, because it is so unlike other examples of faith; not because it resembles them. And so we shall cast no great light on the question, by plugging trivial parallels such as that of the political vote. The difference is, after all, so startling. Belief in God is belief in his existence; belief in the Liberals involves no such affirmation. The Liberals exist, in any case; 'Worse luck!' you may add, if you deplore the splitting of the white-collar vote—for it takes a whole white collar to meet round the neck of an English prime minister. What the Liberal voter affirms is that the Liberals are worthy of trust; that is the subject of debate. Whereas no one who is not hysterical or deranged debates whether God or the devil is to be trusted. God is trustworthy, by definition, always supposing that he exists.

The difficulty of religious faith may be put in a nutshell. How can an attitude of trustfulness, evidently appropriate to God if he exists, be appropriate to a decision whether he exists or not? I can trust him if he exists, how can I trust him to exist? Imagine saying to the Horatio in Shakespeare's play, 'Horatio, you are such a trustworthy man, I am sure we can trust you to exist; you wouldn't go and let us down by never having existed.' Either he exists, or he doesn't—either Shakespeare invents him, or draws him from the life.

The absurdity we have expressed is so flagrant, that it has led to the denial of any faith-element in a conviction of God's existence. This used to be almost the official Roman Catholic view. We believe in God (it was said) by force of reason; by faith we trust the promises he gives us through accredited channels of revelation, once they are accredited; our acceptance of the channels as authoritative cannot itself repose on faith. Such is, or was, the high and dry scholastic doctrine. As a positive account of the matter, it is utterly useless, and we have already shown why. It is useless, because it involves us in accusing all well-informed atheists either of mental imbecility or of intellectual dishonesty, or of both. As though their disinclination to believe in God were on all fours with the bias I feel against the tax-inspector's estimate of my liability. I tell myself that it cannot come to so much; but facts and arithmetic will persuade me. If they will not, then I am a wilful self-deceiver, or an incapable reckoner, or both. Now I am simply not prepared to bring an accusation of this kind against my godless friends. Since I myself believe, I must suppose that they suffer from some bias in disbelieving; but it is not the sort of bias that turns away from cogent reasons. It is just that subtle and elusive bias which leads to misjudgment in matters of faith.

So we cannot say with the scholastics that faith only comes in later, when we trust the explicit promises of God. There is some element of faith there from the start. Yet the scholastic formula is correct in drawing a distinction between two operations of faith. We trust God to fulfil his promises; we cannot, in the same way, trust him to exist. Faith does not work in the same way in the two cases. And perhaps it might help to have another word than faith to describe our initial attitude in believing God's existence. But until we can think of

6

a word for the job, let us go on saying 'faith', while trying to distinguish one sort of faith from the other.

The faith we are speaking of is a deeply felt personal attitude, even if it is not exactly an attitude of trust. Let us look for an example which might be in some way parallel.

There is a stock scene of Victorian fiction—I do not know how many times it occurs. The seeming orphan, brought up by a hard-faced aunt, is suddenly confronted by his real mother. The mother does her best not to give herself away; but a sort of warm, pinkish wave of sentimental electricity tingles through the child; he is strangely moved, he knows not why. Nonsense, I say; ten to one, the child would experience nothing. Undisclosed, actual mothers can be encountered by seven-year-olds with equanimity. What cannot be a subject of indifference to them is the suggestion of a possible mother, if it actually comes to mind. Our orphan child, let us assume, has some access to normal families. He knows what a mother is. Then one day he says to himself, 'Goodness! Suppose I really have got a mother! They say she disappeared in the Revolution, when I was brought to America. They say she was killed, but I wonder!' The child's mind alternates between hope and resignation. The suggestion that there might be a mother is not an isolated factual hypothesis; it is a picture of the world, with an attitude built in; it is filial existence in place of orphan existence.

In much the same way, the suggestion that there is God contains built-in attitudes. We are too much inclined to think of a disputed idea as a drawing over there on the blackboard, a bloodless diagram about which you and I are calmly deliberating whether to fill it in with the colours of real existence, or not. Such an account is always misleading, but not always equally misleading. It is supremely misleading in cases like those we are considering. For the child, to think of a possible mother is to experiment in having a mother; to try filial existence. The experiment takes place in the realms of imagination, but it is real enough to the heart. And similarly to think of a possible God is to experiment in having God. The attitude of creature to Creator, of doomed mortal to immortal saviour, is built into the very idea. The heart goes out to God, even to a possible God; whether we should call the attitude 'faith' or something else, is a question of little consequence.

That thought of God, from which faith could conceivably spring, is a contested affirmation; it is not a matter of mere curiosity, or of poetic contemplation, like the figure of a nymph in a dead mythology. If the human mind were absolutely single and unitary, like the mind of God himself, we could not make contested affirmations; as it is, the loose texture of our mental life allows us to do so. I say 'There is God', and a piece of my heart goes with it; I add 'Perhaps', my state of being changes; I go on 'But then . . .' and my attitude swings into the opposite. Which of my thoughts, which of my attitudes, is I, or speaks for me? It is notorious that I may be deceived in thinking myself committed in one direction, when I am really committed in another. But so long as I know very well that I am not committed, I do not think of claiming to have faith. Yet the faith-attitude is there, if it is no more than one posture among several which I try by turns. To have faith in the full sense, I do not need to bring it from somewhere else, and apply it to the idea; all I need to do is to let it have its way, and subdue its rivals.

8

But why should I? Why should I let faith have its way? Not, surely, on its own evidence. The orphan's painful interest in the idea of a possible mother is no evidence that he has a mother. His concern is not traceable to telepathic waves radiating from his mother's heart, and agitating his. It is traceable (I suppose) to two factors, the pattern of nature, and the organized environment. Nature brings children from a womb and feeds them at a breast and turns them to their mothers for after-care; social organization gives shape and development to the pattern of nature. As to our orphan, a woman bore him, family life goes on around him. His deep concern over the mother-possibility is no evidence that he *has* a mother; but only that he had, and perhaps that it is a pity he has not.

Never mind (the believer may say); for in the analogous case of concern over the possibility of God, the distinction we have just drawn does not apply. If we *had* a creator, we *have* a God. A child may have lost his mother, a creature cannot, in the same sense, have lost his creator. God may lose his creatures, unless he makes them immortal; he is eternal, they cannot lose their God.

The sceptical counter to this move is obvious. The comparison, as now refashioned, has lost all reality. As it is a question whether we have a God, so it is a question to the orphan, whether he *has* a mother. It never was a question to anyone, orphan or otherwise, whether he *had* a mother. You cannot run a plausible line in ametrist propaganda, to persuade the human race that its members had no mothers, but that they grew on gooseberry bushes. You can run a plausible line in atheist propaganda, to persuade us that nature, without God, is the sufficient cause of our existence. There can be no ametrist

9

propaganda, and why? Because the general belief in maternity has no more to do with faith, or personal concern,
than has general belief in the movement of the tides. I could
not be a witness to my own birth, but I can be a witness
to as many births as I like. My heart may be ice-cold on
the issue of general maternity—I may not be concerned
in the least; the facts will persuade me, though I may
actually loathe the thought of origin from a woman's
body. Whereas it seems that without a positive attitude
of some kind, I shall not be convinced of God.

Yes, the fact of my birth from a mother, and the fact
(if fact it is) of my creation by God, are certainly very
different facts. All parables are imperfect, or they would
not be parables. Wisdom lies in seeing how far any
comparison will take us, and at what point it must desert
us. The scholastics liked to reiterate the platitude that
while God is all the deity there is, an individual such as
my mother is not her whole sort—she is not all the
maternity there is. Unable to verify my birth from her,
I can turn to the childbearing of other women. If I am
unable to verify my creation by my God, I cannot turn
to the creative action of other Gods. But neither can I
turn to other creative acts of the same God. For God's
creativity is all one, and it underlies the whole of finite
existence in an identical way. God is all the deity there is,
and creation is all the creation there is. I cannot refer
from an obscure example to a plain example; and, in
particular, I cannot refer from the example of my own
creation to the example of any other being's; my own
example is likely to be the plainest I can find.

God's creatorship will have to be appreciated if it is
to be acknowledged; and it will not be any cause for
surprise, if appreciation on our part requires an apprecia-

removed from godhead, and human creativity (so-called) from that creatorship which is the prerogative of God. If, then, our own being is to act as a footprint indicating our creator, he must have somehow made himself felt in the evidence, or spoken through the sign. And why not, since he is everywhere present if he exists at all, and the very thought by which we think him depends on his power and his will? A God could show himself through his creation, and it is the simple conviction of believers that God does. But if he does, he shows through the evidence more than hard-headed calculation could build out of the evidence; and the readiness to accept that 'more' will be faith, or the effect of faith.

Without the readiness of faith, the evidence of God will not be accepted, or will not convince. This is not to say that faith is put in the place of evidence. What convinces us is not our faith, but the evidence; faith is a subjective condition favourable to the reception of the evidence.

When an unbeliever hears what we have just said, he takes it that faith is an irrational makeweight to turn a scale weighted by reason on the other side. The evidence for God, he thinks, is intrinsically unconvincing; it is made to convince by the introduction of a selfish and infantile prejudice. Faith believes what she wishes to believe. The believer remains unshaken by the accusation. To him, the evidence is intrinsically and of itself convincing, but only under conditions which allow it to be appreciated. Faith supplies the conditions. Seeing is believing; but visible evidence is itself of no force in pitch darkness. If the scene is flooded with cunningly selected rays of multi-coloured light, illumination may provide nothing but illusion. If the scene is lighted with removed from godhead, and human creativity (so-called) from that creatorship which is the prerogative of God. If, then, our own being is to act as a footprint indicating our creator, he must have somehow made himself felt in the evidence, or spoken through the sign. And why not, since he is everywhere present if he exists at all, and the very thought by which we think him depends on his power and his will? A God could show himself through his creation, and it is the simple conviction of believers that God does. But if he does, he shows through the evidence more than hard-headed calculation could build out of the evidence; and the readiness to accept that 'more' will be faith, or the effect of faith.

Without the readiness of faith, the evidence of God will not be accepted, or will not convince. This is not to say that faith is put in the place of evidence. What convinces us is not our faith, but the evidence; faith is a subjective condition favourable to the reception of the evidence.

When an unbeliever hears what we have just said, he takes it that faith is an irrational makeweight to turn a scale weighted by reason on the other side. The evidence for God, he thinks, is intrinsically unconvincing; it is made to convince by the introduction of a selfish and infantile prejudice. Faith believes what she wishes to believe. The believer remains unshaken by the accusation. To him, the evidence is intrinsically and of itself convincing, but only under conditions which allow it to be appreciated. Faith supplies the conditions. Seeing is believing; but visible evidence is itself of no force in pitch darkness. If the scene is flooded with cunningly selected rays of multi-coloured light, illumination may provide nothing but illusion. If the scene is lighted with good plain sunlight, it simply gets the chance to reveal itself.

Well, but we are not talking of ocular evidence. No man has seen God at any time. We are talking of intelligible evidence. And again, we are not talking of sunlight, we are talking of a mental attitude. How then can the parable apply? It may perfectly well apply; and this brings us to the second point we proposed to develop. For we are all familiar with regions of intelligible fact which are only perceptible in the sunlight of a favourable attitude. Sympathy does not create the personal facts it descries, it reveals them; and there are many true facts sympathy appreciates, to which suspicion closes our eyes. I am not denying that sympathy lies open to imposture, or that suspicion is a necessary guard. I am saying what everybody knows—that the place of suspicion is secondary and subsequent. Without the initial venture of sympathy, suspicion has nothing material to criticize. I may justly suspect my own sympathies; but I must have them first. To speak of sympathy for God would, indeed, be an impertinence; we may however dare to speak of openness, or acceptingness towards God.

The comparison between knowledge of God by faith, and knowledge of mankind by sympathy, is like other parables; nothing is more instructive about it than its inadequacy. Only consider the dissimilarity of the matters compared. We understand our neighbours through our common humanity; we are the same sort of animal, we are reared in the same culture. Failure of understanding through lack of sympathy can never be entire. We cannot fail to see that, behind the phenomena of their actions or utterances, they are men to themselves, as we are. We cannot fail to understand the plain sense of much that they say, or the plain intention of much that they do. We may fail to see the soul, the charm, the kindness, the subtlety—our picture may be cruelly impoverished, but an outline will remain.

Whereas God is not the animal that we are, nor an animal at all. We do not share an identity of nature with him, but are the remote offprints of his likeness. To acknowledge the infinite Creator in the facts of finite existence requires therefore a positive attitude, an incipient faith, from the very start. What is required for an appreciation of the godlike in our fellow-beings is required for any recognition of God whatever. The blind eye of suspicion may reduce our neighbour to a cunning beast; it can utterly shut out the being of God.

But is it not a cruel and an unjust fate which makes the acknowledgement of God depend upon the forthcomingness of faith? If this is the knowledge supremely worth having, how unreasonable that the lack of faith should preclude it! Yes, if faith were a capricious visitant; no, if faith is natural. The knowledge of humanity which is supremely worth having is denied to cynicism and mistrust; no one calls this an injustice, because sympathy is natural, mistrust and cynicism are vicious. That is not to deny that some men are so warped by circumstance, that they are cynical or mistrustful by no fault of their own. And so it is true that many men are incapable of faith. They can be cured, however, and God will cure them, whether in this life or hereafter.

In the sense required by the present argument, faith is natural, for it is no inexplicable or occasional visitant of the human mind; it is built into our human predicament. But there are so many senses in which we would not call it 'natural', that we had better list them if we are to

avoid misunderstanding. First, and most obviously, it is
not natural to the human *animal*; it is natural to the
human spirit at a certain level of development. Until
there is the capacity to think of a sovereign Power, it
would be foolish to talk of natural faith in any sense that
concerns us. Second, it is not natural in the sense of
effortless, as resentment of injuries is called natural in
contrast with magnanimity. It is natural as certain virtues
and duties are said to be natural; the acknowledgement
of them arises out of our common predicament, though
the exercise of them requires what is called 'character'
in a man. Third, it is not 'natural' as lying on one level
with our concern for the natural (that is, the created)
order. Faith is no more a natural attitude, in this sense,
than theology is part of natural history. Faith cuts across
that obsession with the natural world which has the name
of 'naturalism'; it breaks into another dimension, the
rootedness of the natural order in God. Compared with
the dimension of nature, we may fairly call this dimension
'supernatural'. Yet it is not unnatural to man, since man
is no mere part of nature. Through reason and free choice
he partakes of the divine likeness, and has a 'natural'
concern with the Creative Will.

Faith seems, in the only possible sense of 'natural',
supremely natural to herself; and, if she is to claim
validity, must claim to be natural to mankind. Since she
is felt to be unnatural by numbers of men, she is bound
to view them as the victims of an unnatural habit, which
has become in them a 'second nature': an ingrained
prejudice, a subconscious resolve to count God out, an
unacknowledged voluntary blindness. If it be asked how
such a distortion can have taken hold, heaven knows
there is no lack of explanations. The corruptions of faith

herself are so many and so appalling as to allow atheism to pass for illumination. The evidence of faith is that it convincingly shows us things in their true colours; having once seen man in God, we know that we have seen man as he is; we can never again believe another picture of ourselves, our neighbours, or our destinies. But superstition and bigotry can so darken and blind the eyes, that nothing is visible in its true colours, or, indeed, with any colour at all; superstition is a night in which everything is either black or else invisible; and atheism or so-called humanism is the very break of day compared with it. But the aversion from faith need not be motived by faith's corruptions. Men turn from faith, because to acknowledge God is to acknowledge *my God*, and men either hate, or fear, to admit that they have a God, or that there is any will sovereign over their own. If they do not fear God, they may fear to be deceived, in wagering their existence on uncertain hopes.

Both the scandal of faith, and the force of it, lie in the fact that the (possible) God of our belief must be *my God* to each of us. Apart from the implied relationship, there is no field in which the peculiar action of faith can be deployed. It is this that makes the absurd banality of the common comparison between faith in God, and the readiness of a scientific investigator to assume an hypothesis. The action or being of God can actually be handled as a hypothesis in a scientific argument; but then, so long as a scientific level of treatment is maintained, there is no place for the attitude of faith. And why? Because the God of the hypothesis does not appear in the guise of 'my God'. If, for example, an act of God is tried as an explanation for the beginning of the world process. Then the name of God is a mere pawn in the game of cosmological chess. The God-pawn may keep its place on the board, or it may lose it, being captured by the forces of the rival argument. The man is interested in working out the game, he is not interested in one piece more than in another; he is not experimenting in the faith-attitude, he is solving a problem according to the rules. The God-hypothesis is maintained, and proceeded upon, to see what it is good for in a given field of explanation; there is no flicker of faith towards God. And why? He does not appear in the guise of 'my God', but only as the possible explanation for a train of events.

What I have just written is, as I can see, terribly indiscreet; I give myself bound into the hands of the Philistines. Everyone is going to exclaim, that we cannot hope to think fairly or to think straight, so long as we are engaged with a disturbing and emotionally charged idea, the idea of 'my God'—the possibility that I have a God, or rather, that God has me for a creature. Whether the idea attracts or alarms, the emotional racket is equally loud; I can't hear myself think. The first move must be to disinfect, to objectivize the idea; and that means considering it in a context which isolates it from all this 'me' and 'mine'.

By all means (we will reply) let the evidence for religious beliefs be stated as objectively as it allows of being stated. But how objectively is that? God alone has access to the life of God in God; his creatures will scarcely claim to know anything of him, but through the part he plays in creaturely existence. God cannot be known simply as God; he must be known, if at all, as the God of . . . 'Very well,' you may say: 'but why as the God of *me*?'

At this point I find myself driven to make an avowal

which will, I dare say, be regarded as utterly discrediting. I am going to admit that all genuine evidence for God's existence reckons in the quality of human existence, and that if we take ourselves out of the picture, the evidence vanishes. Take the most abstract argument that can be stated for God as the cause of the world. You would say, would you not, that if the argument is valid, it would be just as valid, had there never been men at all. It professes to take the form 'No God, no galaxies' or, if you like, 'No God, no gas—no God, no anything.' What have the special qualities of human existence to do with the issue?

I reply, that however abstract, however scientific, such an argument is made to sound, the scientific colouring is largely irrelevant to the theological conclusion. The argument really is, that nothing can exist in the finite, changeable way without depending upon an eternal and boundless existence. We can narrow the issue still further: the whole argument is about the single word 'exist'. How can I know that to *exist* (in the changeable and finite way with which alone we are directly acquainted) is to require a changeless and infinite Cause? I shall need to have some insight into *existing* before I can argue like that. And where shall I find it, but in my own case? We credit existence to the galaxies, and rightly; we experience existing in ourselves.

We can argue to God from the galaxies—certainly we can; we can endeavour to show that, impressive or far-spreading as they are, and unimaginably old, they need God in order to exist, just as much as we do. 'As much as we do'—that is it; unless we could extend to the galaxies, by however remote analogy, the existence we have in ourselves, we should not even know what we mean in saying that they exist. To prove the God of the galaxies is to prove the God of existent creatures, and of existent creatures I am the type. I cannot prove the God of the galaxies without proving my God.

If we say that the base of the argument for God's existence is an argument drawn from man's existence, we make ourselves an easy target for ridicule. Aren't we taking ourselves a little too seriously? The God we need to prove is the God of the world; and what is man's place in the world? Pre-human history was ten thousand times as long as human history has been; and post-human history may be ten thousand times as long again. Even while we are here, what is our part? Are we not dust upon the star-dust of illimitable space? And how is it that we come to be here at all? We are the most casual of by-products. As fungus grows in rotting trees, so life is parasitic on energies breaking down. Here we have a splendid theme of stock rhetoric. I could keep it up for hours, and so could you. But enough is enough. For all these sounding rhetorical buffets are aimed at shadows.

If we argue to divine existence from human existence it is not because we take man to be the crown, glory and end-product of the universe. It is the weakness of our faculties, not the strength of our position, that leads us to take ourself as standing instance of created being. It has, of course, to be admitted that we have one privilege: we can raise the question about God's existence. Mountains and hurricanes, suns and planets cannot. Not even dogs, nor dolphins even, though high claims are being advanced for their discursive powers. Are they not being kept in tanks on the other side of the Atlantic, and trained up to talk to the Man in the Moon? But however it may be with dolphins, we at least can reflect upon our existence. We cannot, on the other hand, get outside our own skins, there lies the infirmity of our condition; so when we philosophize on the world's existence, we must be content to take our own for sample.

Yes, theology is about man and God; about God as the creator and saviour of man. But man is not so slight a basis for theological belief, either, if, along with man, you reckon in his roots. What I am directly aware of, what I acknowledge as dependent upon God, is my existence. But it will be silly of me indeed if I credit myself with existing in unitary isolation. I may be a mushroom sprung up in a night—as we said, like the fungus on a rotten tree. I might not have grown; the tree could have done without the fungus; but not the fungus without the tree. No tree, no fungus; and no soil, no rain, no sunshine, then no tree. If you know God as your Creator, you know him as the creator of everything in which your being is rooted. To make you or me, God must make half a universe. A man's body and a man's mind form a focus in which a world is concentrated, and drawn into a point. It may be in that point that I know existence; but it is an existence which involves the world. And so, as we said, to argue from our existence as men to the existence of God is not to take so slight a basis, after all.

The qualifications are important; but, however qualified, the statement stands; theological belief is concerned with the creator of man. That this is so is obvious, if we consider what God is taken to be. One of the silliest of all discussions is the question whether God is personal—it would be as useful to enquire whether ice is frozen. The theological question is not, whether the world depends upon some sort of exterior cause utterly undefined in nature; the very question would be meaningless. The question is, whether the world depends upon a supreme creative will; and that is the same thing as supreme person. Now if God is inevitably and always thought of as supreme person, he is no less inevitably thought of as the supreme archetype of man; for where else, I should like to know, are we to look for personality, if not in ourselves? We have not yet learnt to talk to the Man in the Moon, nor even to the dolphins in the tank.

To sum up: it is in ourselves that we sample that existence, of which we see the cause in God; and in ourselves that we sample that personality which furnishes the idea of God. The basis of theology comes down to this: human existence has a superhuman creator; the God of my belief can only be my God, and the attitude of faith is necessary to any genuinely theological contemplation. We may be wise, rational, or calm in the exploration of this, as of any other relationship; but unless we open ourselves to it, we shall not be convinced of him to whom it relates us.

In conclusion, let me recall that the faith I have been attempting to describe or to define is that initial faith, which ought not perhaps to be called faith; that attitude of openness or responsiveness through which we move towards an acknowledgement of God's existence. Of such faith we may say, that the mere fact of our moving towards belief is a sufficient sign of its presence in us. But such initial faith is not the faith that saves; it is not enough to believe the existence of God; 'the devils also believe, and tremble'. It is not even enough, to make belief predominant, to commit ourselves to it, to enthrone it above rival attitudes; we must honour our belief in God by giving God his due; and God's due is our life. Indeed we shall not achieve full intellectual belief unless we live by it. Who can go on believing in a supreme Good which he makes no motion towards embracing?

Union of will with God is the subject-matter of revealed religion; we may believe in God, but how shall we walk with him unless he comes to walk with us? Here is a topic which we cannot open in this present chapter.

The practical element in belief is so vital, it has led Christians to say that faith is a purely practical matter, a willingness to trust God and to do his will; and that consequently all worries about the objective truth of theology are a waste of time. This, however, is an exaggeration so absurd that it is amazing it should impose on intelligent men. Say, if you like, that what is asked of a learner-alpinist is that he should obey the guide's instructions and put his weight on the rope; say that these are practical matters; say there is no need for him to have a theoretical understanding either of weights and stresses, or of the way ropes are made, or of the principles on which the guide takes his decisions. Very well; but he must take the rope to be a rope, that is to say, a flexible cable of sufficient strength; and the guide to be a guide, not an impostor or a criminal lunatic. The factual correlates of a practical attitude may be simple, but they are no less essential for that reason. In the matter of religious belief they are, indeed, more important than my mountaineering parable would suggest. Religion is more like response to a friend, than it is like obedience to an expert. It is enough to know that an expert is an expert; it is not enough to know that a friend is a friend. Response, by definition, aims at being appropriate; the more understanding we have of the object, the better we can respond.

If the practical demand is what gives reality to belief, it is also what adds goads to fear. The horror of God is the horror of being enslaved. Like so many positions on both sides of the theological debate, it begs the question. If God is the creative spring of all being, and the inexhaustible fountain of all newness—that is, if God is God—one is no more enslaved by dependence on him than one is enslaved by the habit of breathing. If, on the other hand, God is an idol of the human mind, one is enslaved by obsession with so tyrannical an idea. What is a *free-thinker*? Not, I suppose, a man who maintains freedom of mental manoeuvre by refusing submission to true facts. Freedom can only be freedom to embrace and explore the world; not even the humanist can create his universe; he must respond to realities according to the demands they make on him; and it cannot surprise him that, in the eyes of a believer, the supreme freedom should be freedom to know God and to respond to him. 'How cramping, to shut oneself in to the God-hypothesis!' Yes, if God is a hypothesis; but if you think so, you are assuming that he is not God. To the believer God, like man, is a reality about whom all sorts of hypotheses have been, and can be, entertained; the variety of the hypotheses does not debar us from practical response to their object.

Is the acceptance of God as my God a cramping acceptance? Well, is the acceptance of my neighbour as my neighbour a cramping acceptance? X married a wife, kind and clever and better than he deserved. X deserts her in the midst of her second pregnancy. His wife cramps him; he wants to be off with a fascinating blonde.

She cramps him, for she puts a limitation on his freedom of action. But she exists, and so do her children. She loves him (blast her!) and the children need a father. Besides, he gave his word. Reality is a nuisance to those who want to make it up as they go along. But then, while every wife is actually limiting—she is a finite good; there are charms she doesn't possess, and another will—God does not limit us by being limited; he only limits us by being true.

# Providence and Evil

How the goodness of God is reconcilable with the occurrence of numberless evils is a question which is meat and drink to the hecklers in Hyde Park. 'Is God good? Answer me Yes or No. Is he almighty? Yes or No, please. Would a good person ever let innocence suffer if he could help it? Oh, he wouldn't, wouldn't he? Well then, why does God . . .' The topic is meat and drink almost equally to such of the humanist philosophers as bother to discuss theology at all.

I will hope to deal with the Hyde Park wrangle presently. But before I bring Providence and Evil into relation with one another, I mean to say something about Providence on its own account. Are Christians committed to a belief in God's general providence? And if they are, what is the ground of that belief?

To start with, what is Providence? The word, like so many words, has been spoilt. It is used flippantly, and it is used solemnly. It, or its by-forms, will be used solemnly by men who offer you insurance policies. The Provident Society will insure you (at a premium) against all the ills to which flesh is heir—or so you believe, under the hypnotism of the sales-talk. On reflection you may notice a few omissions—sin, unhappiness, war, sickness, and death. But these are trifles. Financial providence has got all the essentials perfectly taped.

So much for the solemn use, which, it will be observed, is severely secular. The theological use is predominantly flippant. 'I got the dates mixed and went to tea with Barbara on the wrong day. It was really a providence, though; for Barbara was out and there was the most marvellous girl in her room, using her kettle.' This is a joke. No one is meant to suppose that it was the special contrivance of the divine will you should disappoint Barbara, or should put yourself in the way of deserting her for a new flame.

But theologians talk seriously of Providence. What do they mean? Do they mean that by the help of good angels, most accidents turn out fortunately? That if we are easy-going and somewhat careless, we shall secure advantages which care and foresight would frustrate? Or do they go more by the analogy of financial providence? Do they mean that God somehow takes care of those marginal difficulties which cannot be controlled or met by a little man handing out insurance cheques? That neither sin, unhappiness, war, sickness nor death will be allowed to embarrass us? But what can be the use of saying so? We sin every day, and bitterly regret it. Many people are terribly unhappy, some are incurably ill, all suffer at last the supreme object of natural terror, physical death.

What is the solid core of a Christian's faith in Providence? When we say that God exercises providential care, we undoubtedly mean that he takes thought for his creatures. He does not simply throw the energies of nature into the arena of space and let them fight it out. On the contrary—we trust the Maker to do the best for those he has made. Only in trusting God so to act, we need not trust our ideas of how he will act. Any belief in Providence must admittedly consist of two parts; a general belief that God will take care; and some sort of suggestions, however sketchy, of the form his caring may take. No one would claim to believe in Providence without having any such suggestions in mind. Nevertheless, the fundamental part of the belief is faith in divine care itself; the conviction that God is omnipotently good, and that his good omnipotence bears upon the world in all its detail. As to the ways in which it comes to bear, we may be more or less agnostic.

What we have first to do is to show how belief in a providence bearing upon particular persons and events is a consequence of any tenable belief in God whatever. I say, any tenable belief; for there are several beliefs about God, and not all of them are tenable. There are Jews, Christians, Mohammedans, there are polytheists, Brahmanists, Buddhists; they all believe something, but they are not all equally wise. So what I shall do is to make some remarks in support of two contentions: (1) that theism of the Christian type is the only creditable sort of theism and (2) that it implies belief in Providence.

In raising the topic of many religions I may seem to be digressing too far from the matter in hand, but I will hope to be forgiven, because the topic is itself of perennial concern. We wish to claim that religious belief is natural; and we point to the fact that most men hold it, anyhow until they are argued out of it by a dubious sort of intellectual sophistication. But we no sooner observe that most people hold it, than we observe that they contradict one another about it. Are they all equally wrong? How are we to tell which of them is right?

Let us try to bring the question under control and make it manageable. A rhetorical statement about religious diversity will be most picturesque if it counts in cannibals and Hottentots. We will take leave to cut them out. The infancy of the human mind conceived infantile theologies. Those who entertained them could not think about anything, to call it thinking; least of all about supreme being. We confine our attention to the religions of man's maturity. The Greeks, indeed, were polytheists but, as St. Paul very justly told them, they came to know that they ought not to be.

Even when we are rid of the Hottentots the diversity which remains still looks unmanageably great. But we can make a further drastic simplification. Judaism, Christianity, Islam, Buddhism and Brahmanism differ from one another in two quite distinct ways, and only one of the two need here concern us. They differ about the very conception of God, or of the world's relation to him; and they differ about the points at which God has specially shone through and become apparent to mankind. An example of the first type of difference is the opposition between pantheism, which somehow fuses the world with God, and transcendental theism, which makes the world the creature of God. Examples of the second type of difference are conflicting claims for Mohammed, Moses, Gautama and Christ as being the supreme revealer. Now for the practice of religion the second type of difference is enormously important. It is all or nothing for a Christian, whether or not he is right to follow Christ. But theoretically this sort of difference is far less fundamental. There is no reason why a Mohammedan should differ from a Christian, let us say, over the doctrine of creation. And disagreements of the second sort are also less of a scandal. It seems very natural that peoples with different histories and settled in different countries should have met the divine in different historical manifestations. (Not that this will stop their seeing, when they come together and compare their beliefs, which manifestation has the highest claim.)

By contrast it may strike us as surprising that mature religions should differ in the very conception of God as God of the world, and God of man. It is indeed surprising; but for all that, we need not be hopelessly at sea, unable to make up our minds which theology is the better. For in dealing with the questions basic to all theology, rational criticism can do much. We can deal with the issues on their merits, and without reference to the claims of rival revelations.

The grand division is between pantheism and theism, India and Israel. As for Buddhism, which claims to be godless, it arose as an agnostic heresy within pantheism itself. It retains the character of a religion by holding on to the ghost of the pantheism about which it is so negative. There is no difficulty in stating Buddhism in such a way as to cut it off from any doctrine of reality whatever; but that is to make of it a practical ethic and nothing more. (Our atheistic humanists also have an ethic; but it is a mere abuse of language to say they have a religion; unless, of course, they are religious in spite of themselves and against the logic of their own principles.) Buddhism is either a hesitant witness to pantheism, or no witness in the case at all. And we can say so without in any way belittling the value of the Buddhist ethic.

How are we to decide between theism and pantheism? On both sides there is a recognition of supreme being; but one party places it above the world, the other identifies it with the stuff or substance of the world. Can we make a choice? We can perfectly well do so, and on rational grounds. It is a sound principle, surely, that nothing should be asserted about the mysterious realm of the divine, which contradicts or undermines what we know about the natural and the human. Now I know my own personal being, and my neighbour's, far more sharply and clearly than I can hope to know the divine nature. It is preposterous, then, to advance a doctrine about the relation of your being or of mine to the divine life, such as to infringe that personal distinctness which I so certainly perceive in us. I am myself a person, a moral agent, responsible to God if you like, dependent upon God if you like, but never to be merged in the existence of God. A pantheist theology falsifies what we most manifestly know. A theology which is going to allow finite beings to appear in their natural colours and to be tasted in their vivid reality must make every individual thing the world contains distinct in substance from the deity which supports it.

The scientists of the last century seemed eager to bar God out of the world, that they might make the world safe for science; and in a way they were right. The sciences study nature, and they have reason to insist that nature should be natural. They will not accept a theological, that is to say, a personalized account of the natural order. If a scientist accepts a theology of nature, it must be a theology of relation (nature hangs upon God) not a theology of identity (nature is God).

We ought not to brush away either the scientific naturalism or the personal realism of western thought as mere regional idiosyncrasy. They are acquisitions of the human mind which can never be abandoned; and they join hands to place the world outside the personal being of God. It is easy to view such a tendency as a movement in the direction of virtual atheism. Is not the Sovereign of the Universe being treated like the Mikado of old Japan? The politest of gestures may bow him away into a place sealed off from the exercise of real power. The Shoguns of natural force are to run (as it were) the politics of the world; the divine Emperor is to be honoured with all titles, and troubled with no decisions.

Ah, but the Mikado was no more than a man, the divine titles were but flatteries; his sovereignty was created by the breath of adulation. God is an actual omnipotence, and by setting the world outside his own being he assures his freedom of action in respect of the world. The world is so made as to run itself, but every creature it contains is confronted by the omnipotence which made it; is confronted, that is to say, by an inexhaustible power for good, and an inexhaustible fund of invention or contrivance.

The sun, in the height of a clear moon, radiates on every earthly thing that lies open to his light; and so a transcendent Godhead must radiate on every creature subject to his will. All things are external to his being; nothing is outside the sphere of his action. And it is the present relation of every creature to almighty Goodness, that makes the core of the belief in Providence. A machine-gun runs out of bullets, the sun does not run out of rays; everything within the field of his effective radiation is touched by the darts of his fire. And why? Because the solar rays are not darts at all; they are active relations immediately springing into existence between the sun and any centre of force within the area of his influence. It is physically impossible for anything to exist in the sun's region of space, and not be linked with him by a line of living light. There is no such thing as mere coexistence between the sun and any element of his environment; there is always a live relation, an instantaneous flow of fire. And similarly, though nature is created to act of her own motion, there is no such thing as the mere coexistence of any part of her with the being of God. If anything exists, the divine Goodness radiates upon it.

When we compare God with the sun, it is the utter unlikeness of the things compared that makes the splendour of the parable. The universal radiation of the sun is the monotonous operation of a physical energy; the inescapable sovereignty of God is a distinct attention of personal will bestowed upon every existent creature. To compare God with the sun is to say something like this: 'Think of it! There is a mind which does not swing the beam of its attention about, like the revolving beam of a lighthouse, picking out one object after another; this is a mind which simultaneously and perfectly attends to all things.'

Are you brave enough to believe in God at all? If you are, you are bound to digest this bewildering fact: God cannot be God, he cannot differ from us in the essential way which makes us finite and him infinite, unless his mind is infinite too; and an infinite mind cannot conceivably be liable to preoccupation. For us men, attending to one thing means disattending from another. The universe queues up for its turn of our attention, and most of it will go home disappointed, like nine thousand in a crowd of ten thousand who thought they would shake hands with the Queen. The Queen has only two hands, and she is not expected to shake with more than one of them. We have a restricted power of attention, or of thought, and we do well if we bring the half of it to bear most of the time. But God is God; he is a being and a life infinite or unlimited; he can and does give an entire, an adequate and an undivided attention to every single creature and every single circumstance.

It is not silly, childish or superstitious to suppose that God attends to your prayer or your conduct like a parent watching an infant when the parent has nothing else to do. It is merely to credit God with being God. What is silly, childish and superstitious is to imagine that, in giving you the undivided attention of his heart, your creator will forget his other creatures; that he will be ready to disregard their interests, or the very laws of their being, while he arranges little providences for you, all leading to lollipops.

Properly speaking, there are no problems or difficulties for God. He sees the answer in seeing the question. But he makes a vast synthesis of facts in forming his will; and if we are to have a lively picture of his providence, we shall be obliged to paint in human colours; we shall have to imagine what it would be like for us to exercise providence if we were where God is. The vast synthesis of fact, the bewildering balance of competing interests, would present us with a mountain of mental labour and an agony of awkward choice; and so we see as a difficulty what for God is just a multiplicity. Let us accept the limitations of human language, and venture to speak of the difficulties confronting God's providence. But we may still maintain that the difficulties lie on the side of the world, not on the side of the Divine Nature.

There is no difficulty to be overcome, in God's achieving a simultaneous attention to all things in all their detail. The difficulty is presented by the criss-cross of forces and interests in a world of creatures.

Even though the difficulty is no difficulty for God, it is still a limitation. The world is such a tangle, God cannot do for each of his creatures here and now what (we feel) he would wish to do for it, if that creature stood alone. But why should Almighty Goodness make the world a tangle or, if he made it straight, why should he have let it tangle so? Why should the works of an almighty power get out of hand, or present problems to their own creator? When we ask questions such as these, we realize that we are on the very verge of getting beyond our depth, if we are not out of it already; so we had better plant our steps with some caution, treading first where we can feel the firmest ground, and seeing how far we can advance. For we do not suppose that we shall know everything, even at the furthest stretch we can manage—not everything about the mysteries of infinity, and of the divine purpose.

In doing theology it is always vital to build in due order, consolidating first the positions or the truths which come first to our knowledge, and making them the foundations for the rest of the structure. We must not dig up our own foundations in the process of enlarging our house. It was on this principle we proceeded just now, when we were discussing pantheism: we decided to consolidate our knowledge of finite personality and of natural substance first, and to build up such an account of infinite personality and of divine substance as could rest upon it, without dislocating our basic natural knowledge. And now the same principle must be observed in thinking about the riddles of Providence. We must consolidate first what we know first and best.

And what does come first in our knowledge? An acquaintance with this natural world of ours, just as it is, and imperfect as it is. And what comes second? The great theological perception that the imperfect depends on the perfect, the finite on the infinite, the world upon God. And what comes third? A realization of what God's infinite perfection means, and a corresponding trust in him to do the best for this imperfect world, as it actually exists.

You will see that these three moves form a circle and round off the subject. We start with an imperfect world; we fall back on God, its origin and support; we come forward again with God's saving providence, to better his imperfect world. All three positions are concerned with actualities. What sort of a world is this world of ours? On what Cause, on what God, does it every moment depend for its present existence? What does such a God actually do about such a world? Not only are these questions about what is actually going on in some sense; they are also practical questions for us. What God is actually doing is a pattern into which I can fit; indeed, it is the pattern into which I must fit, unless I am a misfit.

But now we proceed to ask a fourth question: Why God, being perfect, should have given the world the flaws or imperfections that it has. This fourth question has the innocent air of being simply one more step in the same path of enquiry. It is nothing of the sort. It breaks out of the circle of actualities and attempts to find a footing on the ground of might-have-beens. For to ask why God made the world like this is to ask why he did not make it otherwise. It is to institute a comparison between an infinite range of supposed possibilities and the universe it has pleased God to make.

What are we to say of such a question? First, that it is superfluous to the other three. We can understand our present world without answering it. We can be assured of God's goodness without answering it. We should cast no light on the present working of his providence, however we were to answer it. Second, we can do nothing with the question anyhow. All our reasoning and speculation is based on the world God has made. What worlds he should or might have made is not man's question. It is or was God's question. We can do nothing about it. He has (humanly speaking) done something about it, for he has made the world he has made, and not some other sort of world. I can no more think myself out of this world than I can jump off my own shadow. I can think outwards, painfully and step by step, from the place where I am; struggling out towards the bounds of space, or back to the great Cause on which all things depend. But if, in imagination, I divest myself of every human and bodily circumstance, and place myself at the springing-point of possible worlds, in the untrammelled choice of all-sovereign will, then what can I make of it?

We have no business with defending God for having made this world rather than another. We may defend him, if we think it necessary, from the charge of creating a world which was not worth having. Yet who can take such a charge seriously? The suicide, in the moment of his black despair, desires to be relieved of his existence. And why? Because he is deprived—

deprived of the health, or the companionship, or the scope of action which belong to human life in this world. His complaint, whatever he may say, is not that existence is a curse, but that he is cut off from its blessings. The very intensity of the indignation or the grief which we feel over the affliction or destruction of God's creatures is a testimony to the esteem in which we hold the happiness and the mere life of the creatures affected. To call the world an evil world is meaningless rhetoric. For the world is the only field of values with which we are directly acquainted. We are bitterly indignant against the disvalues, and rightly; for mental grief, like physical pain, finds its function in making us detest the evils which God would have us resist or cure.

But why, we may ask, are the disvalues there to start with? Must we still accuse God? Does he act like the malicious neighbour in Christ's parable, and scatter tares among the wheat? No, the comparison does not apply, for evils are not *things*. They are unhappy states or misdirected acts of creatures having the capacity for pleasure and for success. Evils do not exist, they happen. They are not created, they are incurred.

Still, why incurred? The question is as old as any mature reflection on these matters; we can see the influence of it in the biblical account of Creation. I suppose that the first words of Genesis mean something like this: 'When first God created heaven and earth, the earth was all anyhow and darkness was over the deep. But the breath of God fluttered the face of the waters and God said, Let there be light.' The 'all anyhow', the *tohu-bohu*, the chaos, is overruled by God, but it continues to make itself rebelliously felt; if we had no experience of it now, we should have no reason for saying that it was 'in the beginning'. There is a recalcitrance still, an obstinacy in the material on which the divine craftsman works. Other peoples went as far or further than the Hebrews in acknowledgement of the chaos-factor; indeed, the inference is well nigh inescapable. It is a familiar predicament with human craftsmen, to be let down by the material in which they work; the clay crumbles under the modeller's hand, or it cracks in the heat of his oven. Nature, like the craftsman, seems to find her whole positive tendency in imposing a rhythm or a shape; only the shape does not always take, nor the rhythm always fulfil itself.

Very well; but why should an almighty creator choose a treacherous medium to work in? The ancient world, which produced these reflections, had nothing solid to offer in solution of the difficulty. The modern world is more happily placed. It is commonly thought that physical discovery has made theology harder to believe. Here at any rate is a point at which it has made theology vastly more credible, and thrown a brilliant light on a dark place. The ancients could see no sense in the disobligingness of the material factor, because they took so negative or passive a view of it. It was, as I have said, as though the divine artificer were working with a coarse and ill-mixed clay. Modern physical enquiry shows us that the lowest elements of nature are not thus passively lumpish. If they can with difficulty be persuaded to keep in the rhythm of higher organizing forms it is because they are so busy being themselves at their own level. If we are to use a simple human analogy, we may prefer the statesman to the modeller or potter. Why is it hard for the statesman to impose forms of political or economic order on multitudes?

Because the component individuals are busy living their own lives and providing for their households. He can only make his large-scale organization work by diverting the spare energy of individuals into the running of it. He must persuade them that co-operation with the system imposed will forward rather than frustrate the purposes which as individuals they entertain.

In some such fashion we may say that God respects the action or organization of nature's elements; he does not violate it by the higher levels of organization and higher modes of action he superimposes. Now in the political sphere a hundred per cent success for public order or for economic planning is unthinkable, so long as individual freedom is given its rights. So in the natural world a hundred per cent success for animal bodies is unthinkable, if the cellular, chemical and atomic systems of which they are composed are to retain their rights, and go on being themselves in their own way at every level.

When we contemplate the physical creation, we see an unimaginable complex, organized on many planes one above another; atomic, molecular, cellular; vegetable, animal, social. And the marvel of it is that at every level the constituent elements run themselves, and, by their mutual interaction, run the world. God not only makes the world, he makes it make itself; or rather, he causes its innumerable constituents to make it. And this in spite of the fact that the constituents are not for the most part intelligent. They cannot enter into the creative purposes they serve. They cannot see beyond the tip of their noses, they have, indeed, no noses not to see beyond, nor any eyes with which to fail in the attempt. All they can do is blind away at being themselves, and fulfil the repetitive pattern of their existence. When you contemplate this amazing structure, do you wonder that it should be full of flaws, breaks, accidents, collisions and disasters? Will you not be more inclined to wonder why chaos does not triumph; how higher forms of organization should ever arise, or, having arisen, maintain and perpetuate themselves?

'Yes, of course,' you may answer. 'I never doubted that the world was a marvel of creative skill; and I do not dispute what science has so clearly shown—that it is all alive and going; there is no passive clay, no dead wood anywhere in it. But I should still like to know why God rooted the higher forms of existence in lower forms, with all their inevitable stupidity and mutual disregard; or why he gave these lower forms freedom to run themselves, instead of moving them like pawns on a chessboard.'

If you raise such questions, I shall be driven to the rudeness of telling you that you do not know what you are talking about. You suggest that God might have made some such higher forms as he has made, without rooting them in the action and being of lower forms. I reply, that we have no power to conceive anything of the kind. And as to your suggestion that natural forces might have been kept in divine leading strings, I can only say that, so far as I know, running oneself one's own way is the same thing as existing. If God had made things to exist, but not to run their own way, he would have made them to exist, and not to exist.

There, then, is the world, and I do not know how to

complain of it. I detest its evils, and I do rightly; my detestation is a reaction meant to arm me against what Providence is set to mend. For over against this complex world there stands omnipotent Goodness, radiating on every part of it.

We have still to ask what providential care does for the world it confronts. I should first like to say that when we speak of Providence we are simply speaking of God, or of God's action. The habit of dividing the divine government into departments is at the best a convenience, and at the worst a nuisance, of human speech. We are not called upon to show that heaven runs a Ministry of Providence with a separate staff of angelic executives, quite distinct from the Creation Office or the Preservation Office or even (if it is decent so to speak) from the Court of Atonement. And in any case Providence would be a strange title for a separate organization; rather as though Parliament were to institute a Ministry of Ways and Means. Ways and Means to what? Providential contriving of what? Providence means 'foreseeing care'; to say simply that God exercises providence tells us nothing about the ends he brings about, nor even the means that he employs.

God's providence, therefore, must always be seen as the accompaniment, or the instrument, of more definite aims; and first, of creation and preservation. Though a thousand species have perished with the mammoth and the dodo, and though all species, perhaps, must perish at the last, it is a sort of miracle that the species there are should have established themselves. And how have they established themselves? Science studies the pattern, but theology assigns the cause: that imperceptible persuasion exercised by creative Will on the chaos of natural forces, setting a bias on the positive and achieving the creatures.

So providence is an aspect of creation itself; a creation not finished in six days but perpetually proceeding. Are we not ourselves in process of being created? Young people, obviously; who knows the person each will finally become? Even those whom the eyes of youth see as set, finished and irredeemable are not all such fossils either; do you think these pages I am here composing are the playing over of an old record? The author becomes a different thinker by thinking his way through his paragraphs. It is, indeed, in ourselves that we best see the operation of such mysteries. Every sparrow is an individual, unlike every other; and the special thing God makes in that sparrow is the product of all the special circumstances concurrent in her production. Most of us have little insight into the singularity of sparrows. We can do better with the human case. For you to be what you are involves a universe; and if your being what you are is the work of God, then an infinity of events was under his hand. It was his skill to draw you out of the genetic pattern of your ancestry, the culture of your time, and the complex of relationships surrounding you. This is not to deny that had your ancestors been more temperate, your parents wiser, your teachers more conscientious and your school-fellows not such little beasts, you would have been a better person than you are. Yet, such as you are, God made you; and the supreme prerogative of the divine art is to draw good even from evil. Not a greater good, no; we do not help God to produce a better thing by offering him worse materials. But what he makes is always a unique good. You are you, and no one just like you. The defects, as well as the advantages, of your background have gone into the composition of the mixture.

Providence, then, is the function of creation; it is the contrivance by which God makes, preserves and enriches ever new existences in face of a world of creatures already in position. Of what else is Providence the function? If not of creation, then of salvation. Those of God's creatures which are salvable, he saves.

It is absurd for any Christian to undertake a defence of God's good providence, or to justify his tolerance of the evils he permits, without speaking of a resurrection. 'Come now,' says a sceptical antagonist, 'the resurrection of the dead is the supreme improbability. You can't expect me to consider that, until you have shown me the prevalence of divine goodness in human affairs apart from any such hopes. Bar out the life to come, and strike the balance of God's dealings with mankind, without it.' Shall I take up the challenge? I might as well agree to box with my wrists tied. How am I to strike the balance of God's dealings, if I leave out that single weight outweighing all which he has flung into the scale, his own godhead clothed with flesh, drawing us into the fellowship of immortal being? We cannot interpret the ways of God if we falsify them; and it never was his purpose to let perish any creature in which his likeness was so far realized, as to make the immortalization of such a creature meaningful. Immortal dogfish are no more to be looked for than immortal dogroses. But where there is a mind able to abstract itself from the mere concerns of its body, and to take its stand, as it were, on the steps of the all-surveying

Throne; a mind able to look out through the impartial eyes of God, to share his concern for the common good of his creatures, and to love the fountain of that good in God himself; where there is a mind capable of such things (and the capacity is in all of us) it was never the purpose of God to let such a mind perish, unless it were through its invincible perversity. So we will not dream of justifying God's ways with men, if we are obliged to leave out of view the very highroad of his goodness, immortal hope.

Can we do nothing, then, to meet those who disbelieve immortality as yet, and ask to be shown a goodness in God which may help them, after all, to hope that he may also raise the dead? Certainly we can. We can show the providence of God in creation and in animal happiness; but then we must show that the balance is reversed, if spiritual creatures are the prey of death. We can show that a natural faith in God, inclining us to trust his goodness, must acknowledge itself mistaken, unless it can accept his revealed promise, and look for a raising of the dead.

But we do not only wish to say that God prevents the triumph of evil by saving souls created in his image. We wish further to say that in saving mankind God works by way of providence; he works, that is, through a care for all the detail of our lives. It should be no figure of speech to the Christian, when he prays 'to do all those good works, which God has prepared for him to walk in'. In making us anew for immortality, God does not simply give us a gospel of general promises and a law of general precepts, nor a general credit of grace in our spiritual account, to meet spiritual expenses from time to time incurred. He makes us a path to walk in and the particular grace to walk in it. Every circumstance of life is a divine call; for God's providence makes it the special means of his and our glory.

I will now make a very general remark. When we look at the circumstances of our day, and hope for the action of God's providence to get us through, it is natural we should wish him to act as we should act if we could; that is, by altering what we see before us, perhaps removing an obstacle, perhaps mending a bridge. But God's supreme skill lies not in manipulation on the existing level, but in drawing some new thing out of existent states of affairs. Even Christ began to pray in Gethsemane for the removal of the Passion from his path. The divine will did not remove it, but brought the new life of resurrection out of it. When God removes evils in the human sort of way, it is commonly by the employment of human hands. His own divine way is to make unthought-of goods out of permitted evils, and to triumph by new creation.

The folly of discussing goods and evils is notorious. Nothing that can be said in cool reason offers any consolation to the sufferer, and nothing that is said in general will speak to the particular case. The example of Gethsemane may remind us that disasters cannot be surmounted until they are met, and that every grief, like every temptation, provides faith with a fresh battlefield. Temptation cannot be conquered by wholesale resolution, nor will philosophy draw the sting of suffering beforehand. But when all this has been said, the Christian will wish in moments of calm to understand as far as he is able the ways of God, and the sort of discussion we have conducted has its place. Let us summarize what we have tried to say.

Belief in Providence springs from a belief in God's transcendence. We cannot be pantheists, because pantheism collides with natural certainties. If we are theists, we set omnipotent goodness over against the world, to radiate upon every part of it, and to master it for its good. If it be asked why a Providence which mends the world did not make it such as to need no mending, we answer that the question conceals and involves another question, Why God made this world rather than some other; and this second question is one which we neither need to ask nor indeed are able to ask. Taking the world as it is, we see that its faults and flaws are no gratuitous scattering of tares among the wheat, but inseparable from its positive character; a character we cannot think away however hard we try. Such being the world, God's providence acts upon it for continued creation and conservation, and in furtherance of redemption. We will not dream of interpreting the scope and effect of God's providence, if the Christian's faith in redemption and immortal life is excluded from the scene.

# Creed and History

PERHAPS we will be expected to approach the subject with a parade of open-mindedness, asking, to begin with, why we should look for any revelation of God in history at all; and then, if indeed we are able to satisfy ourselves on that head, proceeding to snuff about the fields of time until we start a fox—that is, a divine revelation—and having started it, hunt it down the centuries until it yields up all its secrets to us, and turns out to be the well-known gospel fact. We shall do nothing of the sort, however; the pretence of setting forth without a scent or clue, and of beating the field for game, is so manifestly insincere on the part of a Christian theologian, that he can scarcely expect a patient hearing if he tries it on. We know all the time what the great discovery is going to be; it is like reading a mystery tale after having looked up the final pages. As I do not wish to insult the understandings of my readers, I will take it as agreed that we are talking about the revelation in Christ. The question is about the nature of its setting in the world of historical fact.

In the two previous chapters we have reflected a good deal on the vast fabric of the universe; and in such a connection the most glaring paradox of the Christian revelation may be the minute field to which faith confines its decisive occurrence. That we may lose

47

none of the force of the objection, we will entrust it to a soap-box orator, and give him full rein.

'I will concede you for the sake of argument,' this critic says, 'that the Almighty reveals himself in human history. And I will deal handsomely with you—I will not simply concede that the great Cause and Maker of all shows through his human creations, as he shows through all his handiwork. I will concede that he reveals his mind to us men quite particularly, and of his own special motion; that he speaks to us through chosen lips, and deals with us in marked events. I will concede that he does so from time to time, as the occasion may seem to require. But you will not be satisfied. You wish to speak of one final revelation. Nor does that satisfy you, either. You must have it that God's revelation is a man, and to this man you assign a third part in the mysterious Trinity, which is the divine life above all worlds. How can you do so, without claiming for our little globe and its inhabitants a central place among the almost infinite galaxies of stars? It is in vain for you to plead that mere size, mere space, is nothing; that quality, not quantity, is the first considera-tion here. For what right have you to presume man's qualitative uniqueness? How do you know that God has not many races of rational creatures as good as mankind, or better, tucked away here or there in the enormous folds of space? Their claims on the divine favour will be as good as ours. Why should a man, born on our little earth, be honoured with a third part in the Godhead? Is it not a pathetic piece of parochialism to suppose it?'

We can feel nothing but gratitude for so clear an unmasking of absurdity as this is; and we can welcome the opportunity to agree that if Christians wished to give a man, once born on earth, a third part in universal Godhead, the monstrosity would be as great as our critic suggests. We do not, in fact, want to assert anything of the sort. We should not have known the Trinity, if one of the Divine Persons had not become present with us in Jesus Christ. The Trinity would, however, have been the Trinity just the same.

Let us consider, then, the general bearings of a belief in the Trinity and of its relation to the historical person of Christ. As I said above, we forswear any pretence of starting from open evidence and hunting doctrine home. I will not ask how we first reached a belief in divine Trinity, but what the belief is, and why we continue to hold it. After that we will see how it was that Christ revealed Trinity to us; and having reached that point, we will hope to deal with our critic's difficulties.

We will begin by recalling the admission we made in our first chapter, that theology of the Christian type is cosmic personalism. If we cannot see the reasonableness, and indeed the necessity, of accepting our personal being, our mind or will, as our clue to the supreme cause of the world, then there is no theological question to be discussed. We must take it that mind or will comes before all. But not solitary mind. It is a mere superstition to suppose that we know of such a thing as mind in isolation. Mind is a social reality. The characteristic act of mind is to discourse. Real discourse between persons comes first; the mimic dialogue of solitary thought is secondary; the thinker, by a fiction, represents the other in his own mind and talks to himself. The fiction is a temporary expedient, convenient for certain purposes; condemned to our own conversation for any length of time we begin to feel somewhat unreal, and not a little mad.

It is true, of course, that personal reality exists in individual centres, or foci, alone. The Englishness of the English is a way of being human; it is common to many, but it is actual in each of us, not in a mythical Britannia transcending or permeating us all, and provided with a mind of her own, not to mention a shield or a trident. English nationality is a vast complex of relationships and mutual influences; but the real points which the relationships relate, the centres which both exercise and undergo the influences, are Tom, Dick, and Harry; for they are the foci in which the English life exists. But the complementary truth is equally unmistakable: neither Tom, Dick nor Harry exists as a person, apart from the complex of relationships focused in him.

But are there not hermits? There are. Yet even hermits talk to God; and even hermits were talked into talking, and loved into loving, by men, before ever they took to the wilderness of their solitude. Their fellow-men exist for them, through memory and imagination, still; through prayer besides. A hermit is a man who, under the bewildering conditions of our common life, believes he can keep God and man in better focus, and more truly related, by some withdrawal from human neighbourhood. No hermit, I hope, thinks he will be a hermit in heaven; or supposes that his final happiness would be greater, if he was. Every civilized mind seeks an occasional and temporary hermitage. How did I write this book? I got away from the company which is, in general, the breath of life to me, and wrote. Yet I wrote for my readers; some vague image of the sort of person I meant to address floated before my mind; or how should I have composed a discourse which, however ill-judged it may be, has its whole being in the relation between the writer and his public?

A word or two of jargon is sometimes serviceable for summarizing a paragraph of statement. Shall we say, then, that mentality, as we know it, is *plurifocal*? But now theology is the conviction that mind, infinite mind, is above and before all things. Are we then to say that the mind of Godhead is plurifocal too? We might shrink from the conclusion; for precisely the difference between God and us must surely be that we are many, he is simply one. Your mind and mine are each embodied in a separate lump of flesh, and the two lumps are mutually external to one another. Huddle together as we may, we cannot occupy the same volume of space. Whereas God is neither embodied, divided, nor scattered, he is perfectly one. How should there be any plurifocality about his personal entirety?

How indeed? And yet there is another side to the argument. The grand rule of theology is this: nothing can be denied of God, which we see to be highest and best in creaturely existence. Now in us, personal relationship is as valuable as personality itself. Friendship, mutual discourse, common action—these things are as valuable as the power to think and to feel; without them, we might scarcely care whether we could think and feel, or not. How can we deny mutual relation in the Godhead? God is love; not only loving to ants like us, but related by relations of love on his own level.

The doctrine of the Trinity does not pretend to make God intelligible. It lays down certain requirements. It says that if God is to be God, the Godhead must be at once more perfectly one than any one of us, and allow also for a mutual love more outgoing than is found in any two of us. We do not know how these seemingly opposed requirements are fulfilled and reconciled in the Godhead; we only know they must be. If we wish, we may define the divine level of being as that level, above all our conceiving, where unity of life and discourse of mutual love most perfectly combine. I hope you will see that this is not an empty speculation, a pretence of knowing what cannot be known. God is whom we worship; we worship the sovereign unity, we worship the infinite love; nor do we worship two realities, we worship one God who is both.

One cannot justify, or explain, a distinction of persons in the Godhead, without showing that it is a better doctrine of God than any other; and that, in spite of its paradoxical form, it makes the highest sort of sense. But if it does make sense, just as a doctrine of God, it is abstractly conceivable that we might have thought of it for ourselves, simply by working upwards from the human image to its divine archetype and apart from any revelation through Christ. In fact it did not happen. Christ revealed the Trinity.

It may be useful here to draw an analogy from physics. I am scandalously ignorant of the science; I gave myself many headaches in my student days trying to understand Einstein's general theory of relativity. I could not understand most of it at all, but I did think I got hold of his definitions of space- and time-relations by lines of real force. I understood them, because they are self-evidently true, they make sense. The old definitions accepted by Sir Isaac Newton and his followers were not merely incorrect, they were nonsensical. It is not merely that Einstein's very special and advanced physical observations proved that this isn't a Newtonian world. You couldn't have a Newtonian world. It is no blasphemy to say that God himself couldn't have created such a system. Why, then, was not the Newtonian theory of space- and time-relations long ago exploded, and the Einsteinian substituted, by sheer hard thinking about the nature of such relations? Why did it require an encounter with very special facts about the crooked movement of light rays to force a supreme intellect into an acknowledgement of the obvious? Why indeed? Yet that is what happened. It is easy to be wise after the event; no one succeeded in being wise before it.

So the Christian theologian is wise after the event; he sees that only a Godhead containing distinction of persons can be the creative archetype of the person or mind we know in man. But no one was wise before the event; it took the impact of the divine Son incarnate to make us acknowledge the Father and the Son in spiritual relation.

I know that what I have said about the divine persons is so inadequate as to be almost useless; but I hope it is just sufficient to give us what we need for an answer to our critic. He complained that by making an event once occurring in our tiny corner of space central to the life of Godhead, we were mistaking the parish pump for the Albert Memorial. Our answer is that what happened in the first thirty years of our era was central to our life, not to that of the Godhead. It happened to us, that the life of the Blessed Trinity was so thrust upon us, and brought into our midst, that we stopped ignoring it.

So far, so good. But what are we to say about our critic's hypothetical races of rational creatures, tucked away here or there in the voluminous folds of space? Ought we to be fitting out missionary space-ships, to go to the back of the galaxies, and carry them the gospel? Or has God dealt with them through some different dispensation? What is the use of asking questions we cannot answer? A believer must suppose that God will take care of his own, wherever they are. How he has dealt with us, we partly know; how he has dealt with them, we cannot so much as guess. Of one thing only we can be certain; whether they know it or not, God is their God and the Trinity is their archetype. For whatever we may find at the back of the galaxies, we are not going to meet with solitary mind. We may meet races widely different from ourselves; but if they are rational, or capable of God, they live in mutual converse, and express by their dealings one with another their transcendent model, the Trinity of Persons in Unity of Godhead.

In his planetary romances Dr. C. S. Lewis indulges a Christian imagination on the subject of God's ways with the inhabitants of other worlds. *Out of the Silent Planet* and *Perelandra* not only display a heavenly gift of concrete fantasy, they contain much theological wisdom written in between the lines.

> Go aboard. I will leave you and Lewis in orbit;
> With him for your pilot, perhaps you'll
> Encounter the Martian mind, and absorb it;
> I'm backing to earth in my capsule.

For I have still much to do on the terrestrial plane. It is not enough to site the Incarnation of God in a speculative field of perhaps populated planets. We have to place it in the solid and ascertainable context of human history.

We spoke just now of the gospel events as central to our history. They were central in importance, so far as concerns our relation with God. They were central in no other way. History has no middles, just as it has no beginnings and no ends. That shining milestone, the year 1066, was no milestone to those who passed it. History just goes on and on and on. Very likely it will stop, but we do not know when. If God was to visit us for our salvation, incarnate in a man, he must do so at some one time, and every time is a casual time. The inevitable randomness of a physical world was the subject of my last chapter. This world is a world of accident, of sheer brute fact. If God was to put on a coat of flesh, the coat was sure to be made of casual stuff. He could not be a man-in-general. In fact he was a Galilean carpenter, turned freelance rabbi. He could not be born at all times, or places; he was born in Palestine in the reign of Caesar Augustus.

Christ's life, then, may be called the centre of history, only in the sense that the horizontal movement of human affairs was uniquely touched at that point by a vertical inflow from above. We must resist the temptation to make the lines of secular or cultural history converge on Bethlehem or Calvary, and radiate again from there. Most of the lines which merit the attention of historians passed by on other roads. Christ was scarcely a historical figure, any more than you are, or than I am. Apart from the brief episode of his arrest and execution, he

55

walked largely unnoticed between the feet of governors and kings. He overtook public history after the event, when the Church became a social and at length a political force. Then the world looked back in amazement, and wondered that the incarnation of God should have left scarcely a mark on secular records. Did Pilate keep a day-book? I suppose so. And what did his clerk enter on that fatal Friday? 'Jesus of Nazareth in Galilee, condemned to the cross on the High Priest's accusation, for claiming the kingship. He confessed his guilt.'

Yet however far from the focus of public history Jesus moved, the human existence of Jesus was a focus drawing the world into itself. To say so much is to say no more of him than we must say of ourselves; were we not remarking in a former chapter, that if God wished to make no more than any single one of us, he would need to make half a universe? And why? Because no one of us would be the creature he is, if a thousand thousand lines of converging history, both physical and personal, had not met in him. Your life or mine is but a half-sentence in the book of the world. Tear it from its place, and it cannot be read; or if it can be read, it signifies nothing. Since God has made us each what we are, our argument was that the material out of which he made us must have been subject to the persuasions of his providence. Without control of the means, he would not have achieved his end. He steered many sequences of cause, many lines of influence to their meeting place in you or in me. And so with the human being of Jesus.

History in general does not have a centre, but the secret history of God's providence in the making of any one creature has a centre; for it finds it in the being of the creature that is made. Most of such histories are untraceable, and known to God alone. As for Christ, we cannot trace his family background beyond the first generation, we know nothing of the village schoolmaster who taught him what he knew. It would be wearisome to catalogue the subjects of our ignorance concerning him. But there is a compensation. Jesus identified himself with the divinest hopes of his nation, and we can trace the line of providence leading up to him through the spiritual history of Israel. For we have the Old Testament.

I do not know how much it is appropriate to say here about the Scriptures; readers who are looking for the commonplaces of scriptural divinity are not likely to look for them in this book. But I will dwell a little on the point I have just made. The Old Testament contains the story of God's secret providence in making the humanity of Christ, in so far as that making worked through the direction of Israel's destinies, the enlightenment of Israel's faith, and the kindling of Israel's hope. This is history of a sort, but not of the common sort. History as commonly understood concerns the acts and thoughts of men, not the half-disclosed purposes of God.

We have a history scholar in our College, a pious man who is often in Chapel, but no theologian. I wonder what goes on in his mind? We begin reciting the psalm; and there we are in the midst of a world where men cry to God, and are delivered from physical calamities; they sin and fall sick, they repent and recover. Wicked men are struck down red-handed by the judgments of God; the piety of good men increases their flocks and herds. The first lesson, being taken from the Old

Testament, assures us that victory lies in the gift of heaven, not in the force of arms, and that a king's political successes or failures are in accordance with his obedience or disobedience to the preaching of ecstatics. What does the history scholar think? Does he think that all history should be written like this, and that academic history is a foolish game one plays to please a tutor, or to get a degree? Or does he think that things used to happen like this in Old Testament days, but do so no longer? Or does he think that the biblical picture is an old-world legend, illustrating sound spiritual principles by means of gross historical distortions?

I should like to lay down the following propositions for his guidance. First, the way God worked through the history of Israel is the way he always works. We have said that God makes things make themselves; his creatures are not visibly overruled; the hand of God is perfectly hidden in the achievement of his effects. Consider the physical creation. If we look back to the bottom and beginning of things, to the first and simplest patterns of physical energy, it is senseless to say that they had it in them to become you or me, by any working of statistical average or self-selection of chance variations. And yet, in the development of natural forms leading up to man, we look for natural causes. The divine leading which draws them upwards is an invisible persuasion, moving natural things to behave naturally. We cannot find a point at which natural explanation fails; or if we do, we blame it on our imperfect science, not on God's abrupt inference. It is the same in human history; it was the same in Old Testament history. Only that in history a new factor may enter. The persuasions of God may cease to be invisible, in so far as men see their minds as subject to the persuasions of God. And such men were the prophets.

The second thing I wish to say is this. Though the way God worked in Israel was the way he always works, there was nevertheless something singular about the history of that people. In general, the difficulty of following the trace of God's providence in history is that we cannot presume to fix the goal of his purpose. You might trace several trains of events which looked providentially ordered towards the emergence of the British Empire in its Victorian or Edwardian form. But perhaps you think that the Empire was a mixed blessing to mankind; and so you might hesitate to write a modern sacred history on the theme of God's work in bringing about the British Empire. It is not that you doubt God's hand to be everywhere in such events. Only you may see his action as a persuasion of our mixed and foolish aims towards an end less disastrous than their natural result. We cannot commonly discern in God's providential government achievements so simply divine that the line of purpose leading to them stands out like a thread of gold. But the life and person of Jesus is achievement as perfectly divine as it is perfectly human; and so the events leading to it have a providential intelligibility not elsewhere evident. As the Apostles saw, Jesus is the clue to the Old Testament; looking back from him, we discern what the leading of the divine purpose was.

The third thing I wish to say is that if our history scholar, reading the first lesson, judges it to be overlaid with legendary distortion, he is perfectly right. History is a science of very recent origin. The ancient Hebrews were incapable of holding the balance between a straight

history of human actions, and a discernment of underlying providences. They wrote the presumed history
of God's leading and they wrote it almost neat. They
had little sense of historical cause and effect. Nevertheless, they were realists after their own manner. The
edifying story of God's providence had to square with
the brutal facts of exile and oppression; it was through
these hard realities that they received God's judgment
on their sins, God's abasement of their pride, and God's
purifying of their aspirations.

The hopes of Israel were set on a divine kingdom; and
if there is one reason rather than another why Christ
came in the reign of Augustus, it will be that his firm
establishment of the Roman Empire made the political
realization of Jewish hope for ever impossible. Though
Jewish fanaticism proved in the mass impervious to the
logic of events, it was possible in such a context for
chosen spirits to accept the transformation of national
ambitions which Christ brought about.

The crucial point for relating history to Providence
is found not in the Old Testament, but in the New.
For it is in Christ himself that the divine action
underlying natural events shows through them most
transparently. The natural medium—that is to say, the
human story—loses all its opaqueness; the life of Christ
no more stands between our perception and the action
of God, than the lenses of a telescope stand between
us and the star on which it focuses. It is not merely that
the life of Jesus, being flawlessly good, shows no
divergence from the divine will willed concerning it.
Were that all, Jesus might have fulfilled his function
by remaining a model village carpenter all his days, and
dying a natural death at a ripe age. It is that the very

action of Jesus is divine action—it is what God does about the salvation of the world. In the common case of a good human life, humanity supplies the pattern, and God the grace. In Jesus, divine redemptive action supplies the pattern, and manhood the medium or instrument. A good man helped by Grace may do human things divinely; Christ did divine things humanly.

Wherever the eye of faith looks in the created world it perceives two levels of action. There is the creature making itself, and there is God making it make itself. Jesus is not unique in the mere fact that the personal life or act of God underlies his action; for nothing would either be or act, if God did not thus underlie it. But the underlying is not everywhere the same or (let us rather say) the relation between the underlying act of God, and the created energy overlaid upon it, is not everywhere the same relation. In the case of mere physical forces, there is the highest degree of mutual externality between the two; it is natural enough to speak of God's action here as the action of a cause. In the case of rational creatures, there is more mutual penetration; the entry of the divine into the human may be called inspiration on the one side, and co-operation on the other. In the person of Christ the mutual interpenetration is complete; it is necessary to talk of a personal identity.

I said that Christ is the crux of the relation between human history and its providential guidance. Does that mean that he provides the clearest instance, or the most difficult instance, of the relation? I feel obliged to say that he provides both. Both the most difficult, and the clearest? How is such a combination of opposites possible? Let me try to explain. The relation between a Maker who makes things make themselves, and their own making of themselves, is paradoxical anyhow for our minds (not for God's, of course). The absolute instance of the paradox is the clearest, or most undeniable instance. It is also the most glaring, and therefore the most difficult.

Let us take for comparison something else which strikes us as intrinsically difficult or mysterious. Suppose yourself called upon to expound what is called human creativity, but which it is better to call inventive genius. What are you going to say about it? There seems in the end nothing you can say. You can trace the materials in the inventive mind, you can lay out the conditions of the problem to be solved, you can record the steps and stages of inventive thought. But the sheer act of invention—you may say that it just comes to a man; and that isn't true, either; the man does it. And now suppose that, scandalized by your inability to explain it, people deny that there is such a thing as this personal and mental act of invention. They want to hold that the reality we mistake for it is an automatic chemistry of ideas, blending into new compounds; or that it is a sort of super-electronic computering. How are you to argue against such wrongheadedness? You may be convinced that the act of inventing is going on all over the place, and in all sorts of trivial decisions or practical constructions made by human beings. But you will find it useless to quote such common examples. For these are just the sort of cases your wrongheaded friends like thinking about, and find it plausible to reduce to mental mechanics. What, then, are you to do? You will have to cite the most astonishing examples. What about Einstein formulating his theory; what about Shakespeare composing

*Hamlet*? These examples are the most evident, because they are the most glaring; but equally and for the same reason they are the most out-of-the-way, mysterious or puzzling.

In the sort of argument I have been recalling, we find ourselves appealing from commonplace examples to the supremely difficult example. And this we do when we want to prove the sheer fact that such a thing as (let us say) inventive genius does occur. But in another sort of argument we do exactly the reverse: we appeal from the high and difficult case to the humdrum level of common cases. We take this course when people say to us, 'It's no use talking about the act of invention exerted by Shakespeare or by Einstein. It is clean out of our world, we haven't a clue to it.' 'Oh, come now,' we reply, 'have you never thought of an original joke? You have the recipe for invention in your own head. I'm not saying that your stroke of wit is as good as Shakespeare's play; but I am saying that it is a piece of invention.'

It is hardly necessary for me to draw out the application of my parable; the reader will have seen what I am at. I want to say that the way in which God works through his creatures at any level is even more mysterious to us, because in this case we have not got the recipe; we are all of us inventors of a sort, but none of us is God. We cannot see how the supreme Maker makes things make themselves. 'No,' says someone, 'and it just does not happen; there is no need to suppose it.'— 'Ah, but it does,' we say: 'look at the example of Christ. There you have God showing through his work.'—'Well, perhaps it looks like it,' comes the reply: 'but then to make out the case, you have to speak of the divine as living and working in the human, in a way that is absolutely unintelligible.'—'Extreme in degree,' we answer, 'but not utterly unintelligible. What happens when we pray ourselves, on the day when prayer comes really alive? Does not a better wisdom and a less selfish concern than one's own take charge of the praying mind? And when it does so take charge, does it displace one's personal will? Of course not; what would be the use? God cannot inspire me, by removing me, by pushing me off the saddle and riding in my place. No, the more I am inspired, the more I am myself; the will God makes me make is my truest and freest creation.' But then again, I may say to myself, 'It may be self-deception after all; can anything so utterly singular occur, anything so out of the course of nature, as that God should make me make myself?' Assailed by such a doubt, I cast my net wider still. 'God *does* make things make themselves. How else should the process of nature, starting from almost nowhere, ever rise to the production of the highest creatures we know?'

Theology is almost wholly concerned with the groundedness of created energies in the action of God. Jesus is the supreme clue, for he is the absolute instance of such groundedness. But if Jesus is the clue to all things, all things are the background to Jesus. A Christian's thought moves backwards and forwards, from the circumference in to the centre, from the centre out again to the circumference. It is thus that Jesus is, as St. John says, the clue to creation itself. 'In the beginning was the Word . . . Through him were all things made . . . And the Word became flesh and tabernacled amongst us; we beheld his glory.' One of the chief

difficulties a Christian meets in reasoning with un-
believers is that they do not see the whole evidence in
that sweep which, to the eye of faith, is familiar
landscape. Isolating the physical creation, they insist on
its brainless brutality, its opaqueness to any providential
interpretation; isolating Christ, they insist on the
preposterous singularity of the claims advanced on his
behalf; isolating prayer or inspiration, the mystical fact,
they insist on its queerness in a world which they wrongly
suppose to be mere mechanism. But the Christian sees
all the works of God, at every level, illuminated and
supported by all the others in a graded sympathy. Christ,
like the sun, casts light on every fact. Christ, like the
sun, too bright to look upon, reveals his luminous power
by the fresh colours he awakens in the wide garden of
the world.

We see that the increase of divine penetration into
creaturely action does not remove, but enhance, the
freedom of the creature. And so, without pretending
to see the mystery of his being from the inside, we must
believe that Jesus is both more human and more fully
himself than any man. Indeed, he makes that impression.
Who more spontaneous in his compassion, more frank
in his indignation, more immediate in his decision?
Everything he does or says comes straight from the
heart. We have scarcely any record of his inner thoughts.
We do not need it; inner and outer with him are one;
what he says, he thinks, what he intends, he does, and
what he expresses, he feels. This is at least half of what
is meant by the sinlessness of Jesus. Where conduct is
blameless outwardly, we suspect that sin may lurk in a
breach between the heart and the hand, or a quarrel
between the thought and the tongue.

The entire humanity of Jesus means that his story would be a piece of historical biography, if we had the evidence to fill in the gaps; we should see him as the man of his time. It is as such that we endeavour to understand him, so far as the evidence will go. It is often said that the traditional interpretation of Christ's person was formalized and distorted by pagan Greek philosophy, imported into the Church. This is, I think, so little true, as to be on balance quite misleading and virtually false. No, the ancient and the mediaeval conception of Christ's person was not poisoned by philosophy; it was starved by a lack of historical sense. Those ages saw him too much in the colourless abstraction of a man-in-general, or in the borrowed clothes of a contemporary with themselves. We see him as a Galilean villager of the first century. The tools of his thinking came from the local stock; only he made a divinely perfect use of them. The Jewish ideas he inherited, broken and reshaped in the course of his life, served him for mental coinage, in the traffic of his unique sonship to his Father, and his assertion of God's kingdom over mankind. He had what he needed, to be the Son of God; as for defining the divine sonship, that was a task for other hands, using other tools; the Apostles began a theology of his person, and the Fathers continued it.

If it was hard for ancient Israel to write the story of God's providence without swamping the fields and hedgerows of historical fact under a flood of pious legend, the difficulty for Christ's immediate disciples was almost greater. How could they tell the story of Christ as the story of God's saving work, how show the divine hand as author of the human events, without swamping natural fact under supernatural myth? Yet the effacement of the

human is so far from complete. that Jesus can still be seen
and known, His human personality, as we meet it in the
Gospels, is certainly no historical novelist's invention.

We cannot discount the possibility of legendary
embellishments; we shall go too far if we assume that
everything supernatural is legendary. What are we to
say of the Gospel miracles? I will present the issue in
the form of a question. The Gospel facts are parts of
human history, though not, as we have said, parts of
public, political or even cultural history. But there is
a sense of 'history' which I need not further define than
by saying that in this sense of 'history' everything is
history which has visibly happened, and which is human.
Now all history in this wide sense is open to investigation
by historical method—a science, or an art, pretty well
understood nowadays. Here, then, is my question.
Ought we to say that no alleged fact of Gospel history
should be accepted, unless it would pass the rules of
probability which secular history would employ? Surely
not. The methods of sifting evidence, or of reconstructing
continuous event, which secular history employs are just
as proper in the field of Gospel history. But what of the
criteria of probability? Secular history gathers its criteria
from a flat-rate survey of humdrum humanity. But the
man of discernment knows that whatever he is dealing
with in Christ, it is not this. For anything we are to
believe, there must, of course, be respectable evidence.
But respectable evidence (in history) is seldom com-
pulsive. We have still to decide whether the evidence
suffices to prove such a thing as *that*. There is much
evidence for Christ's resurrection; but, to judge from
the general level of history and, indeed, of biology,
would any evidence suffice to prove that the dead should

rise? Ah, says the Christian, but to reduce the life, death and—yes—the resurrection of Jesus to the common level, is to beg the case. If Jesus is what we see in him, then he was personally one with the sole bestower of immortality; as John says in the person of Jesus, 'I am the Resurrection and the Life.' To make up your mind whether the evidence for his resurrection suffices, is just one part, but only one part, of making up your mind about the whole matter. To cut off the historical question of the resurrection, and examine it by itself in an aseptic historical laboratory, giving your verdict on it without reference to your general estimate of the truth about Christ, would be nothing but a piece of intellectual cheating. It would not even be good history. History must allow for differences of level. On the dead level of human probability, it was not likely that Shakespeare should write his sublimest works. But he was Shakespeare, and he wrote them.

I see that I am liable to be quoted against myself. For I have worked in general from the principle that God makes his creature make itself in its own way, he does not violate it or force it. And must not the admission of miracle contradict such a principle? In a sense, Yes. The principle attaches to God's general manner of making or governing the world. Nobody who talks of miracle at all supposes it to be a common example of natural order. Exceptions presuppose rules; they do not conform to them, though. But on the other side, no one who believes in miracle wants to say that God *violates* the natural working of the created order by a dislocating interference. It is rather that he enhances, or extends, the action of his creatures; they are able to do what is analogous with what they can commonly do, but goes beyond it. An easy case is the miracle of healing. We know something, and but for prejudice, might know more, about physical effects wrought by acts of spiritual blessing. Nothing natural, then, would be violated, if the healer, strengthened in his blessing-power by unity with the life of God, should do more than we know how to do. Admittedly the tradition contains more difficult examples than the miracles of healing. It may be that some of our written accounts of such events are much exaggerated or confused. They certainly stretch to the limit the enhanced control of mind over matter.

The Resurrection is not a miracle like any other. It is a unique manifestation within this world of the transition God makes for us out of this way of being into another. But no one who believes that God remakes the life of the dead in a new and glorified fashion supposes that he forces or violates their natures in thus fulfilling and transforming them.

The subject of miracle requires a fuller treatment, if it is to be touched at all. And yet I could not see how to let it altogether alone in the discussion of creed and history.

# Sin and Redemption

THERE is no subject about which nonsense has been more solemnly talked in the last forty years, than sin. According to some of our sages, there is no such thing at all. Sin is a bogy set up by theologians to make men miserable and drive them mad. According to others, there is sin right enough, oceans of it; we should be mere ostriches to ignore it. But who (they ask) understands it? Who can cure it? Not the theologian. His theory is mere myth and his practice mere witch-doctoring. The psychologist is the man. He has the factual anatomy of sin, and the scientific cure for it.

The assumption underlying either view is that sin is a spiritual disease, a moral measles. The one party hold that the symptoms are purely hysterical: by dint of telling us that we are all ill, religion makes us ill. We are not ill, however, except by thinking so. The other party allow that the disease is objectively real; organic, as it were, in the psyche or soul. But if so, they argue, it is open like all objective phenomena to scientific study, and amenable, one can fairly hope, to scientific treatment. They will be kind enough to admit that there is some measure of appropriateness in our traditional simples. By long experience, and more by luck than method, the old women in the villages have hit upon cures which have some value against common diseases; and in like manner the old women in the pulpits have hit upon practices which are helpful against sin. But scientific cancer-research will get to the bottom of cancer and scientific psychology will get to the bottom of sin.

Well, but is the underlying assumption correct? Is sin a diseased condition of the human psyche? I find the question one of those awkward challenges, to which one can answer neither 'Yes' nor 'No'. Yes, sin is a diseased condition, for it is certainly not a healthy one. No, for sin is not definable as a condition of the self, whether diseased or otherwise. We cannot say that where a human psyche is messed up or misfunctioning in a given way, there is sin; we cannot (that is to say) define sin in the sort of way we define neurosis or psychosis, schizophrenia or manic depression.

This is not to say that sin is indefinable; it is merely to deny that the definition is a psychological definition. So far from evading a definition, I am about to offer one. Naturally, my definition can only hope to state the basic sense, or root idea. 'Sin' must have many secondary senses, or ramifications of meaning; you cannot hold it against me, if my umbrella fails to cover them all. I shall define the verb, not the noun. Sin, as a noun, describes either an act of sinning, which brings us back to the verb; or a habit of sinning—and that brings us back to the verb again. If we understand the verb 'to sin', we shall understand both the act and the habit.

What is it, then, to sin? It is to do the wrong thing in relation to some person. The prodigal of Christ's parable has sinned against heaven and before his father. He has done the wrong thing by the old man in wasting his savings, and the wrong thing by God in disobeying his will. The definition is not, you will observe, psychological at all. The sinning may have resulted from some sort of mess in the young man's soul; but by saying he has sinned, he is not pointing to any such mess. He may be suffering agonies of remorse, but his confession of sin does not point to this fact either. It would certainly not detract from his sinfulness if he felt obliged to say: 'I have sinned against heaven and towards you, but I'm such a callous young brute, I can't say it costs me a pang.' We are told that he felt the pinch of hunger, but not the prick of conscience. No doubt the harlots in the far country helped him off with his complexes, as fast as they did with his money. He said the decent thing to his father; we have no warrant to suppose that he found the meeting a deeply traumatic experience. The greater his *sang-froid*, the more reasonable his elder brother's disgust, and the more shining his father's unmerited forgiveness.

There is only one element in the definition of sin which can be termed psychological. Sin is *doing* the wrong thing by someone else; and *doing* must be given its full personal value. If a car shoots out on to a major road from a minor without either heed or warning, and you ram it amidships before you can brake, you may be said to have *done* it considerable damage; but only in the sense in which a falling tree or a boulder might be said to have done. You can fairly protest 'I didn't do it; it was no doing of mine'. But when we are said to sin against God or man, it is understood that we are in some measure responsible for the collision. It will be in a very weakened sense, if at all, that a man will be held to sin in violating divine claims of which he is simply unaware.

We will not refine further on the definition of sin. The pursuit of definitions is meat and drink to philosophers, but the taste is not widely shared. It will do for the present if our formula will answer our questions. (i) Is sin a creation of theology? (ii) Is sin a spiritual disease for which Doctors of Divinity might prescribe in competition with Doctors of Medicine?

(i) We may answer the question whether religious teaching creates sin by asking another: Does the inculcation of truth-telling create lying? In a sense, yes, it does; but not in a damaging sense. Teach children to tell the truth, and you make it possible for them to lie, that is, to speak contrary to principles of veracity which they acknowledge. So you create lying. But nobody will blame you. For first, the possibility of abuse lies in the establishment of any standard use. And second, you do not create mendacity or veracity either, as you might create cheating and fair play at Lotto by laying down the arbitrary rules of that game. The instruction you give to the young reveals mendacity and veracity, rather than creating them. Converse with one's fellows is in any case the stuff of life, and deceit is the frustration, candour the fulfilment, of the main purpose of converse, communication. Here are facts or principles valid in their own right. We do not invent them by teaching children not to lie.

Now to apply the parable: we do, in a manner, create the possibility of intentional sin against God by revealing his will. But this is no more than to say that the response for which God's revelation calls is personal, not automatic. Being personal, it is something we give or withhold, make straight or make crooked. The possibility of sin is the possibility of piety, viewed from the reverse side; and the gravity of sin is in balance with the weight of glory.

Then further, we can create neither the claim of piety nor the heinousness of sin, we can only reveal either. Both have their foundation in the intrinsic and always actual relation of a creature made in God's image to its living Creator and willing Redeemer. We can scarcely refrain from mentioning men's sole eternal good, for fear of the painful consequence, that some may turn their backs upon it. If the God of Christians is a fabrication, then sin is a gratuitous annoyance. If our basic theology is true, our warning against sin offers no general cause for complaint.

But though Theology does not, in any mischievous sense, create sin, theologians may well create sins, by falsely defining the positive will of God. Such was Christ's complaint against the Pharisees; they had embroidered the law of sabbath with superfluous comment, until it became a crime to pick and rub corn on your Sabbath stroll across the fields. I once found in the chapel of a girls' school a manual of self-examination, in which the penitent, after considering whether she had feasted on fast days in defiance of the Church, was directed to consider whether she had not fasted on feast-days to spite the Church. Theologians, alas, have invented sins. They did not invent sin.

(ii) To turn now to the other suggestion we had to consider—that sin is a sort of malady open to psychological diagnosis and scientific cure. It is obvious that this cannot be so, if sin is the neglect of a claim, or the violation of a right. Neither psychologists nor any other scientists concern themselves with questions of the kind. Lawyers handle them on a law-court level, moralists on a personal level; but neither moralist nor lawyer aspires to define the claims our Creator makes upon us.

Let it be clearly understood that theology is not warning the psychologists off anything on which they could conceivably lay their busy hands. Any condition affecting the psyche is open to their investigation; and many such conditions, often morbid conditions, arise in connection with acts or habits of sin; a sense of guilt, for example, which ceases to stimulate practical reform, and begins inhibiting endeavour of any kind; or a destructive tension between our ideal projects and our actual desires. About such conditions psychology may tell us much that is of use, and it is great folly in theologians to brush her off on the supposition that the province is theirs, they must know best. Why may not the psychologist do better than the priest in helping a man achieve a happy, sane and generous attitude towards the duties he acknowledges or the derelictions he deplores; whether those duties and offences are concerned with his neighbour or with God, or with what he takes to be his own integrity?

So, then, whatever psychological problems arise on moral or religious ground are open to the psychologist. What psychology cannot do is to determine what is right and what is wrong, what is sin and what is holiness. The analogy of physical medicine may serve here. Take the case of the father of a family. He has a duty to support his dependants by his labour and to help his overburdened wife at home. Very well; but he over-works and comes under the hands of his panel-doctor. What can the doctor do? He can help the man meet the strains of his position; he can show him how to economize and distribute his energy. He can warn him that, if he overdoes it working on his house as well as his job, he will break down completely; and nothing

can be less helpful to his wife than that. All this the
doctor can do. What he cannot do is prescribe the
man a way of life which, from the health aspect alone,
would be ideal. He cannot, for example, tell him to
get rid of his wife and children, throw up his job and
potter round the garden. What is medically ideal may
be morally impossible; for the cultivation of physical
health, important as it is, cannot be the whole aim and
end of existence.

As with physical, so with mental and emotional health.
On the short-term view, it cannot be assumed that what
is psychologically healthiest for us will in every case
answer to the claims of our position; and especially not,
in matters of religion. The acceptance of God's will
for our perfection, and the holding of converse with a
supernatural Being, may impose strains on our fallen
nature not quickly or superficially to be resolved.
Suppose a psychologist were to reach the empirical
conclusion that religion on the whole lessens psychological health, rather than increasing it. What then?
Would he be justified in declaring religion no duty,
and irreligion no evil? He would not, as another physical
comparison may readily convince us. Suppose it were
empirically demonstrated that maternity shortens a
woman's youth and hastens her death—What then?
We should still think it good for her to discharge the
biological and social function which is irreplaceably
hers. Only we should direct the skill of research and
the resources of aid to the lessening of maternal strain.

True Religion, like chastity, may be psychologically
difficult. It is no sufficient reason for abandoning either
the one or the other. But we shall be fools if we do not
take account of the difficulties, and manage them as

wisely as we can. The difficulties are formidable, they are not fatal. God made us, and God is wise; co-operation with his will is not going to have a wrecking effect on our personality. It is going to impose certain strains; and these strains will become intolerable only through our own pride or folly; if we forget that we are men, or that our humanity needs to be managed and considered, even in our pursuit of a divine perfection.

We have now said what we mean to say about the relation between sin and spiritual malaise. We will turn to the examination of a problem which our definition raises. If sin is the neglect or violation of God's claims upon us, then what becomes of the familiar Gospel teaching, that our being brought into right relation with God is a deliverance from sin? Must not the claim reduce to an absurd tautology? Learning music is a deliverance from unmusicalness and marksmanship from shooting wide; so is harmonization with God's will a deliverance from conflict with it. All these things are undoubtedly true, and none of them, it seems, is worth saying. Who does not know that success in any branch of activity is deliverance from failure in that branch?

Yes, but the truisms of theory may be the revelations of life. If I am free to let music alone, my unmusicalness may not strike me as a misery of which musical training would relieve me; but suppose me a clergyman bound to spoil the sung responses of the choir by my daily cacophonies, then the appearance of a music-teacher with the hardihood to undertake so ungifted a pupil as I may well present itself as the hope of a blessed deliverance; and I may apply myself to music more as the escape from misery than as the object of positive interest. So too with marksmanship. If I am Crusoe, forced to live by my rifle on a dwindling stock of ammunition, learning to aim better may present itself as a deliverance from the nightmare of wasting my shot.

No doubt in the end it is blasphemy against God to think of the friendship he bestows on us as primarily a deliverance from sin. It would be like valuing a human friend not for what he is in himself but as a remedy against loneliness. Yet before we have the friend we may be more aware of the loneliness than of any pictured or possible friendship; and before we are reconciled to God we may be more aware of the evil of sin, than we are of the possible bliss of godliness. It could be so; but will it be so? We shall want to make two remarks on this head.

First, our relation with God being inescapable, since we draw our very existence from him, it is not something we are free to let alone if we choose. We violate his will if we do not follow it, we are starved of our supreme good if we do not embrace it. Alienation from God is a positive misfunctioning, a frustration of our total aim. If we are not reconciled to God, we are spoiling the music, we are not just letting music alone.

But in the second place we have to observe that not all actively cacophonous throats are aware of the discord they create, and not all wills in conflict with the divine know themselves to be so. Consciousness of sin implies consciousness of God. It is useless to call upon atheists to deliver themselves from their sin. You must first convince them of God and his holy will. It may not be until they embrace their salvation that they see as sinful the condition from which they are saved. If men are to be conscious of sin before they are conscious of grace, they must have a negative attitude to God before they achieve a positive. In former times there were people by the million who believed in a divine author of the moral law, and knew perfectly well that they were running away from him. The preacher could rub the sore of their sin, and point the path to its cure. But now, anyhow among the sophisticated, the method of arguing oneself out of theistic belief is so current that few men put up with the annoyance of believing in a God from whom they know themselves estranged. Why, they can buy peace of mind and self-deception on the first bookstall they pass. So acknowledgement of sin becomes typical of Christians, who know how to seek renewed forgiveness for it.

The moral subtleties, the psychological nuances here are very fine. Only God knows how far those who find it convenient to disbelieve in him are wilfully deceived. If they are, then they may well have a deep, and deeply smothered, sense of guilt. But there are plenty of genuinely innocent atheists. The bias which makes them so is nothing personal to themselves; it is the attitude of a whole historical phase; it is reaction against the corruptions of religion.

Let us leave the question, how far the state of man apart from Grace is felt as sin, and turn to consider a little more thoroughly what the state is, from which God's grace redeems us. It is one of actual infringement of God's will. The analogy which inevitably presents itself is an offender's infringement of statute-law. But the analogy is more misleading than helpful; the will of God is so utterly different from the law of the land. The law is a set of rules which exist merely by being enacted and recorded. They are not embodied in any live action, unless either we are at pains to obey them, or our disobedience of them is avenged by public justice. The will of God cannot be anything like this; for the will of God is God himself in action, and God is always in action. If I go against the will of God, I do not simply go against a rule which God has revealed for my guidance; I go against what Omnipotence is doing with me, would I but let him. It is indeed the supreme paradox of our condition, that an Almighty Power respects our freewill; but his respecting of it does not mean that he sits back and watches it. He works upon free creatures through all the infinite operations of his providence.

When Scripture speaks of a state of war, a mutual hostility between God and man, it is giving expression to this fact. Modern humanitarianism recoils in horror, protesting that the enmity is on man's side only. The protest is justified, if the purpose is to deny that God is subject to negative passions, or actuated by destructive intentions; the danger it carries is of denying activity on God's part, as well as malice. Between God and sinners there is a real battle of wills. The fighting is let up from time to time on the human side, for sinners have to sleep. It is never let up on the divine side, for God neither sleeps nor slumbers. The divine antagonist may fight like a strong, compassionate man struggling to master an armed lunatic; he fights all the same, until we surrender.

Setting aside conflicts with the divine will on the part of men who know nothing of it, we may distinguish two degrees of conflict between that will and ours. The sharp degree of conflict is where we will *not* to do the will of God as known to us. The weak degree is where we will to do his will in general, but oppose it in particular through ignorance or error. The most tragic conflict of all is where men will to do the will of God in general, or so they think; but their conception of his whole will, and not of certain particulars only, is so false that they are more damagingly in conflict with his purposes than lazy, rebellious or ungodly men might be. Such, perhaps, was the conflict of the divine will with those who procured the crucifixion of Christ.

Only less serious than the mistake of denying any battle of God against us is the mistake of supposing that the battle was called off from the divine side when Christ came into the world, and that some different, conciliatory sort of divine action took its place. On the contrary; the incarnation of the Son of God was the crisis of the campaign and the supremely typical act of the divine strategy. God's battle against us is aimed at two objectives: the mitigation of the harm we might do ourselves or others, and the bringing of us into reconciliation with God. In a literal and earthly war, we may desire both to break the enemy's destructiveness and to recover his goodwill, but the two purposes will be pursued through different trains of action; let us say with guns on the field, and with propaganda over the air. Whereas the battle of the divine will with ours is a battle against our enmity; and when it breaks our opposition it secures our reconciliation.

And how is it done? It has become customary with theologians to let themselves off a plain answer. They will say that the reconciliation effected by Christ's death is an unspeakable mystery, for which a whole series of different parables was offered by scriptural writers and afterwards by the Church; that none of them is adequate, and several of them seem contradictory; we must see what each of them will tell us, and we must leave it at that. I cannot agree. Everything that God does has an abyss of mystery in it, because it has God in it. But in the saving action of the Incarnation God came all lengths to meet us, and dealt humanly with human creatures. If ever he made his ways plain, it was there. The variety of parables express the love that went into the redemption, or the blessings that flow from it. They are not needed to state the thing that was done.

What, then, did God do for his people's redemption? He came among them, bringing his kingdom, and he let events take their human course. He set the divine life in human neighbourhood. Men discovered it in struggling with it and were captured by it in crucifying it. What could be simpler? And what more divine?

In the very brief statement I have just made, I have done what I said was needless, and brought in a parable. That kingship is a parable is evident. God is not king to the world, he is God to it. The parable has nevertheless a proper place in the literal statement, for it was from such a parable that Christ's work began. It was no parable, indeed, to those who first heard him. They hoped that as the Persians, the Greeks and the Romans had in turn held the kingdom or empire of the world, so the people of God should hold it. The hope was crucified on Calvary, it rose transfigured from the Easter Sepulchre.

When we are doing theology, not just history or Bible-exposition, we make it our aim to see truth not as it was provisionally stated, but as it is ultimately revealed to be. God is not king, but God; if, in a parable, he made men partakers of his kingdom, he will, in a more literal form of statement, make them associate with his Godhead. This is not to say that even God's own grace effaces the distinction between what it is to be God, and what it is to be his creature. He alone is eternal, having existence of himself, and in his own right; we exist, and only can exist, by his good pleasure. Even so, we are privileged above irrational creatures, and have that in us which allows of association with the divine.

The two essential capacities of a reasonable creature, to love and to think, are in a manner both divine and infinite. Thought can aspire to think things as they are in themselves, not as they happen to affect the thinker; and this is to model one's mind on the thought of God, the simple truth. So also love can care for things as God made them to be, not as they concern a personal interest, or a private passion. The truth of the way the world goes is the way God leads it, and the soul of goodness in things is their fulfilment of his intention. Our thought and love lack their essential clue, unless we can go behind the great scene and show of things, to uncover the act which makes them be, and the providence which leads them towards their perfection. But no: we cannot go round behind the scenes of nature, nor, if we could, is there anything for us to see. However gifted we were with mind-reading we could not read the thoughts of God, for they are not as our thoughts. There is no mechanism there of statement, comparison, decision, no content of word, image or feeling which we might catch in the beam of our mental wireless, and dream over to ourselves in our own heads. God's thoughts are pure immediate acts of creation, their expression is in the deed done. He uses no mental scaffolding to frame the house of the world; his thoughts are the things he makes.

We cannot think God's thoughts, or love God's loves, in God. But how if he descends to think his thoughts and love his loves in man, and under the human form, through statement, comparison, decision, through word, image, feeling—all the familiar mechanisms of the created instrument? This will be the way to associate us with the Divine activity. The scriptural parable will have its fulfilment: we shall be made sharers in the divine kingship, through union of mind and will with the sovereignty that wields the world. For that sovereignty is of its nature communicable. Before the sovereign thought or love is extended outside the Godhead, it is already extended within it; so God constitutes in blessed Trinity the society of his own life. There is divine sonship by nature, before there is or can be sonship by adoption. There is an equal friendship or association of the Father and the Son, into which the Son may bring us by living as man, and by making us the disciples and partners of his life.

We have been digging a little with the tools of theology behind the parabolic façade, 'divine kingdom'. For, we said, the form in which our salvation was first proclaimed, was of God bringing his kingdom among men. How, then, did he do this? He sent forth the divine life in the person of his Son to live as man; and he began calling men into association with him. Not only did he proclaim that this was the 'kingdom', he showed both by word and deed the living will and action of the 'king'. It was in resisting the action and the claim of divine sovereignty, and in maintaining their own, that Caiaphas and Pilate crucified Christ. They crucified him, and by doing so they gave him the occasion of decisive victory: a victory over fear, error, pride, malice—all the human negatives, all the barriers set up by man against God.

If the reader is already a Christian, and kindly disposed to the line of exposition I have taken, he will perhaps be willing to agree that whatever else may be true or false concerning the Christian faith in salvation, what I have stated is at least true. But, he may say, if such is the basic truth of Christ's atoning action, how are we to fit in with it a very different account of the matter; an account for which scriptural authority can be claimed, but which is more neatly summarized in Mrs. Alexander's line, 'There was no other good enough to pay the price of sin'? Is it true, or is it not, that the sins of men already committed run them into debt with some intrinsic law of justice, the debt incurred being a punishment or forfeit of some kind? And is it true that the score having assumed infinite proportions can never be worked off, as another hymn-writer informs us:

> Could my zeal no respite know,
> Could my tears for ever flow,
> All for sin would not atone?

And finally, is it true that the divine Son took our place, underwent our penalty, and cleared our score?

If you ask whether these propositions are true or not true, and require a Yes or No answer, you force me to vote for the negative: they are not true. But I shall vote with reluctance, because the parable of the hopeless debtor redeemed by Christ's infinite generosity is an excellent parable. It becomes a monstrosity only if it is proposed as a piece of solid theology. Taken as such, it is monstrous enough. The theologian will be bound to ask what he is to make of a debt to a Supernatural Bank of Justice. The idea is utterly meaningless; and if we try to give it substance by personifying the Bank as God himself, we merely exchange nonsense for blasphemy.

Well, but if the parable is a good parable, it must contain more than a few gleams of truth, and we should be prepared to say what they are. And not only that; we claim to have given the proper or literal account of Christ's saving work, and we should be able to show that whatever truth the parable expresses is contained in the literal account. I say, whatever truth the parable expresses, not whatever emotion. The great merit of parable is to convey passion or lay on moral colour; when we break it down to literal statement the colour fades, the passion evaporates. The breaking down is always a thankless task. But we are in pursuit of theological truth; we cannot evade it. So let us proceed.

'There was no other good enough to pay the price . . .' And did not Christ pay the price of reconciliation? We do not commonly think there is anything more costly than death; not, anyhow, for a man in the early prime of his age, living most fully and usefully, and bound by all the ties of affection to living contemporaries; especially if the deprivation of life is exacted by malice, accompanied by ignominy, and executed with torture. If it was thus the divine warrior conquered our enmity and achieved our reconcilement, he paid the price—no question of that. It must be admitted, indeed, that he achieved what he achieved at a price, not by a price, that is, not by a transaction of payment. If, under a barbarous statute now repealed, I were in prison for debt, and you bought me out, you would liberate me not only at a price to yourself, but by the very price you paid. If I were held captive by a remote and savage tribe, and if you went to great expense equipping yourself to effect my rescue, you would liberate me at a price, but not by the price you paid. Your purchase of the equipment would not open my prison by any financial magic.

Let us advance a step further. '*At a price* is all very well, if it is a matter of stressing the cost. But *by the price paid* makes the additional suggestion that the Redeemer stands in for the person he redeems. The prisoner owes the debt; his deliverer pays it.' I agree that a theology which disallowed such an affirmation would be self-condemned. But I ask, Does not the Christ of the victorious reconcilement stand in for those he reconciles? Compare the common case of a personal estrangement, say between father and son; and let it be supposed that the son is entirely in the wrong. Then who ought to bear whatever trouble or humiliation is involved in making it up? The offending party. But human nature being what it is, nothing makes us hate our fellow-being so much as the consciousness that we have wronged him; so it is the innocent party that makes the approaches. If, then, the worthy father perseveres against arrogance and endures disappointment until he succeeds, has he not stood in for his son and done what the lad owed to have done? The comparison is indeed feeble; the Gospel-history outruns anything that any concocted tale will illustrate. For when the divine Son's overtures were rejected by men, they not

only insulted, not only killed him; they said 'We are
the hand of God, our killing is God's justice.' They
framed him for treason to himself, as Charles the First's
too partial apologists said of the royal martyr's con-
demnation. But surely, in Christ's case, the treason (for
there was treason) lay at other doors than his.

'To pay the price of sin.' And what is the price of sin?
Not literally what it costs; say, what the prodigal paid
the harlots. Christ did not pay for us to go on sinning.
Then what price did he pay? What it costs to reconcile
sinners with their creator's will. And what does it
cost? Surely not the serving of a sentence in some
supernatural Dartmoor, or forty lashes of the best. It
costs the abandonment of a false attitude, it costs a
struggle against despair of virtue, a sacrifice of the pride
which attaches us to the defence of our conduct, all
the amends we can make to persons we have wronged—
what else? The catalogue could be greatly lengthened.
Such are the costs of our reconciliation, and such costs
as these are not remitted to us, even by the sacrifice of
Christ. We have all these things to do, only that Christ's
initiative sets us in motion. He took us, and associated
us with his divine life, even while we struggled against
him. He has wrought all our repenting in us.

But still, I think, you are not satisfied, or you ought
not to be; there is still something in the parable of
penal debt paid which our story has not covered. No
Christian can deny or forgo the claim that the blood-
shedding of Jesus was the price of our forgiveness. And
without the theory, however mysterious, of a debt to
the bank of Justice, what are we to make of that? If
there is no score to be cleared before God can forgive,
surely God forgives us in any case, and before he sends

Christ to achieve our reconciliation. What has Christ's death to do with the matter? Only, it would seem, to convince us that if we ever thought God did, or would, withhold forgiveness, we were wrong.

What are we to say to this? Let us begin by recalling who and what God is. God is almighty, and all his action in our regard affects our very existence. It cannot be supposed that God makes mere gestures towards his creatures. What could you mean by saying that he forgives? Surely not that he scratches an entry or pronounces words of indulgence. He who has the power and does not act is convicted of insincerity if he expresses the intention. Since God does not bear grudges, he has no need to set them aside; what, then, can his forgiveness be, but his ceasing to battle against our wills, and taking us into his fellowship? We, thinking by human analogy, will naturally distinguish God's forgiving us from his reconciling us to himself. The forgiveness is what would be, in a man, the attitude; the reconciling what would be, in a man, the consequent action. But God has no attitudes which are not actions; the two things are one. And so if Christ's blood is the price of reconciliation, so it is of forgiveness. And still there is no need for the theory of the Bank of Justice.

But even so, you will not be satisfied—at least I hope not, for you ought not to be satisfied with less than the whole truth. And you will still wish to say, will you not, that God has forgiven all men through Christ, even those whom he has not yet brought into reconciliation with his holy will. Yes; but his forgiving all men through Christ, even the yet unreconciled, is nothing so formal or so ineffective as the deletion of a ledger entry on account of payment received from a third party. God's act of universal forgiveness is the whole train of action he sets working through Christ, through the Spirit, through the Church, through all-embracing providence, towards the reconciliation of the un-reconciled, whether in this world, or in a world to come. And of this great process Christ's blood was, once more, the cost.

I hope now that I have shown two things: first, that the parable about the payment of our penal debt is not the sober nor the ultimate truth; and second, how admirable a parable it is. For it brings into relief several points of great concern, which in the plainness of the basic account might otherwise go unobserved. By the way, I have done a third thing, which I did not (I confess) set out to do. I have not only told my readers the theological truth, as I see it; I have also carried them through an exercise in the way theology is done, and how it works upon parabolic material.

In a theological enquiry, we look for theological formulations. But never let us mistake such formulations for God's revelation. That would be like mistaking a knowledge of Greek grammar for a knowledge of Greek literature. The study of the grammar has its own cool fascination, but it is not the same thing as the enjoyment of Homer or Aeschylus; and its main purpose is, to act as a rule by which to understand such authors correctly. So theology is a rule by which to understand that divine utterance which is also divine action, the revelation of God in Jesus Christ. We do not read the story of the cross to make theological deductions. We draw out our theology that we may rightly read the story of the cross.

# Law and Spirit

I AM no historian, but one thing is clear to me in our island record—King James the Second ought never to have occurred. I dream of what our history might have been if the Restoration establishment had not been knocked to pieces by James's stupidity; if Crown, Church and Parliament had remained in equipoise; if the Church had never been split between a Whig episcopate and a Tory priesthood. Such dreams are uncontrollable, but they are also valueless. What might have been is a vain speculation. Change a single historical fact, and you escape as by a magic door from the world of actualities; in working out the hypothetical consequences you are free to follow your fancy. If what did happen had not happened, then you just do not know what would have happened. Historians who know their trade will have nothing to do with that will-o'-the-wisp, the might-have-been. At the very most, it is a piece of trick-lighting to bring out the shape and colour of what actually occurred. Half the significance of James may be seen in the hopes he wrecked; whether those hopes had a possible future is a vain enquiry.

Of all wild, all fantastic speculations of the sort, the most extreme is the supposition that God's people might have been in such friendship with his will, that the death of his Son was not required to reconcile them. What would have happened? Would Christ have come at all? Surely he would still have come; would

God have made his people suffer for their lack of guilt? Christ would still have come to transform human hope, and to bring men into a more privileged association with their Creator than they could otherwise enjoy. For it is by the descent of God into man that the life of God takes on a form with which we have direct sympathy and personal union. The humanization, the incarnation of God would still have a place, if the heart had never hardened, if sin had not become habit, nor selfishness second nature.

But suppose these happy conditions for the coming of Christ, and what are you to say he would have done when he came? Why anything different from what he did do? For what did he do, but set about bringing men into union with his Father by association with himself? He did not wait to be crucified before he began the reconstitution of God's people round the standard of his empire. Under the actual conditions of human frailty and human revolt, the bringing of men into such a union was not completed without the death of Christ. It was not only that those who rebelled against their king crucified him; it was just as much that those who were pledged to him deserted him. What was it, though, that produced such tragic reactions, the murderous rebellion of some, with the accompanying desertion of others? What but the thing which would, we say, have been the work of Christ in any case, the initiation of the mystical union? He began extending the divine life and will outside his own person, to become the life of others by association; it was against this movement that rebellion was raised, and from this movement that desertion fell away.

It is often said that there is a tension, if not a contradiction, between two expressions of our faith, one in terms of incorporation with Christ's body, the other in terms of reconciliation through his death. The incorporation theology is sacramental and Catholic, the reconciliation theology is Protestant and personal. That Catholics and Protestants have quarrelled is as undeniable as it is tragic. But so far from there being a natural tension between incorporation and atonement, each needs the other and without the other neither makes sense. Christ did not come to get himself killed; he was not a suicide. He came to associate his people with divine life, and they killed him for doing this. By so dying he reconciled sinful wills to God, and made their incorporation in his mystical body a real possibility.

There was a doctrine current among the Jews of Christ's time that Messiah would not come until Israel had prepared itself by repentance and good works. The teaching of Christ was that the kingly presence was bestowed without tarrying for any. His disciples quoted to him the prophecy that Elijah would return to earth and make the people fit for God's kingdom. He replied that Elijah came, and set about his task, but that by so doing he pulled his death upon his head. The same thing, said Jesus, would happen to the divine prince who brought the kingdom itself. John Baptist had paved the way for Christ—he had paved the way to Calvary with his blood. The divine wisdom knew better than to wait for sinners; Christ took hold of such men as he found, and made them fit for himself by letting them betray and crucify him.

That famous slogan of Luther and St. Paul, justification by faith, and not by works of merit, means exactly this: our incorporation in Christ is not earned by our obedience to God. He takes us as we are; what is required of us is trustful and active consent; and this we should be in no position to give, had he not first broken our hard hearts by his death.

We began this discussion in a realm of unreality; and we may wonder whether we have ever quite got down to solid earth. Suppose we admit to our counsels a later and more pragmatic voice than Martin Luther's, the voice of the Age of Reason. Here is a man in black breeches and a bagwig, and this is what he says:

'Fiddlesticks, sir! I say, fiddlesticks, sir! What does any plain, honest man care for your spiritual refinements? I do not say that you have not very prettily adjusted incorporation in a body no one can see, with reconciliation to a person who totally transcends us; and I do not deny that it is harmless amusement for a leisure hour to suppose ourselves the counsellors of Almighty Wisdom, called to instruct Omnipotence whether he should justify us on the score of a faith expressed in good works, or on the score of good works grounded in faith. Here are mighty issues, truly! But while we speculate upon them, the hands of the clock continue to move. We have little time enough to do good in this world; and I would submit to you, sir, that the only certain truth about the will of our Creator is that he did not put us here to waste our opportunities. I would add that he gave us a moral light in the law of our minds, which a wit may pretend to dispute, but only a scoundrel will disobey. The Founder of our Religion, whom I hope I reverence as you do, said many things of necessity bearing upon the circumstances of the time and the foibles of the Jews. But both by example and by precept he published a truth to awaken the moral sense of every people, and of every age; a truth which he placed under the awful patronage of the First Cause of our being, and final Judge of our deeds. Sir, when a man has made himself perfect in the practice of that teaching, I will hear him on incorporation and on justification. He who had done no sin, says the Gospel, might cast the first stone at a woman apprehended in the act; and he who has acquired every virtue may lay the first stone in the edifice of speculative divinity.'

None of us, surely, would be so rash as to incur a head-on collision with the line of so vigorous a contention. But we beg the liberty to examine what it is that our learned Doctor has said. It may seem to us that he has made two points. First, that no speculation on Christian mysteries can be made a substitute for obedience to Christ; and second, that obedience to the teaching needs no doctrinal preliminaries, nor shall we easily find time for them, in view of the pressing calls on our practical benevolence. I will take these points in reverse order.

In answer to the second, I will agree that it is not only needless, but criminal, to make the doing of our acknowledged duty wait upon any consideration, whether doctrinal or otherwise. The teaching of Christ may fuse (as was suggested) into a single force with a man's conscience and claim his immediate assent. Very well then, he must obey it, whether Christ be man alone, or both man and God. Whether or no we have duties to God as well as duties to men, here at least are human duties and we must do them. Nothing can excuse us, and surely not religion; there is nothing more detestable than to make pretended pieties a pretext for neglecting human charities. But Christ, whose moral teaching our

Doctor reveres, asked more of us than the outward deed. He called for that disposition of the heart which can alone make kindness kind or benefits endurable. Our learned Doctor seems to presuppose goodwill; but to presuppose that is to presuppose everything. Is it superfluous to seek communion with the will we obey, that we may share the intention and the spirit, not merely conform to the letter?

And now to take the former point. The fear was expressed that doctrinal definition might be made a substitute for moral action. The fear is just; the danger is always present. But the danger lies in our perversity, not in the nature of the case. We may be content to theorize where we ought to act. But the very matter we theorize demands the action we withhold. We theorize on Christ's reconciling work. But in the living fact, his work of reconciliation is inseparable from the moral truth. As we were saying, he so brought the authority and the love of God to bear, as to produce the breakdown which crucified him, and reconciled mankind. And this action of the divine sovereignty on Christ's world was all one with the assertion of the moral demand. Christ's contemporaries might be puzzled whether to class him as a royal claimant or as a reforming rabbi; a rabbi being by definition an expositor of the Commandments. His disciples might see that he was each in being the other. He was the royal heir of David, but he showed no titles of ancestry. He gave substance to his claim by the sovereignty of his law.

However abashed we may be by our learned Doctor's tirade, we cannot allow him to run a knife-blade between a theory of reconciliation and a practice of moral action. Morality, just as much as divinity, allows of being theorized; reconciliation, no less than law, allows of being lived. The two realities are tied together in the Christian fact; and on neither side are we free to theorize without an eye to practice.

The consideration of Christ's moral teaching is as vital as the understanding of his person to an examination of Christian belief, such as I have undertaken. But it would take us into a detail for which there is no present scope. I must limit myself to broad generalities.

Was Christ a legislator? To some readers of the Gospel, and presumably to our learned Doctor, the salient fact appears to be that Christ gave exact, and exacting, rules for his disciples' conduct; rules which they have been wriggling out of ever since. Other readers are uniquely struck with Christ's denunciation of the religion of rules, that is, of Pharisaic Judaism; did not he condemn it root and branch, as a recipe for turning bigots into hypocrites? He preached (these students of the Gospel say) the free religion of the Spirit; Church-tradition has been turning him into a rule-maker ever since. I will not attempt to arbitrate between these extreme positions; I will simply say how I see Christ to interpret the laws of God, both in the Sermon on the Mount and elsewhere.

We have to see Jesus as a teacher who used the class-room instruments of his time. The Old Testament and especially the writings of Moses provided the text-book. Here were the laws which the God of Israel was deemed to have given, to discipline a fierce and wayward tribe. What was one to do with them? The Pharisaic doctors multiplied ingenious comment, partly to soften, to argue away what was barbarous or obsolete, partly to fit the statute by minute regulation to every circumstance of contemporary life. All this comment Jesus swept away. He said in effect, Take the law as it stands, and ask yourself not, What did God permit? (he may have been grieved to permit it) nor, How much did God exact? (it may have been all that could be enforced) but, What did the Lord who gave each law desire from willing servants, not to say loyal sons? He commands you to love your neighbour; does he desire you to hate your enemy? He directs judges to award exact retribution if a suit is brought into court. Does he desire that suits should be brought, rather than injuries forgiven? He forbids adultery; what lusts does he approve? Honour the sabbath by a holy rest, love your neighbour as yourself. But see, it is sabbath, you are a healer, your neighbour is in pain; what does the God who gave these two commands desire that you should do?

I leave it for you to judge whether this teaching is legalist or anti-legalist. Christ said he was increasing the stringency of written law, by referring us to the very wish of the Legislator's heart. If that is legalism, it is also something more. It leaves us the written law for a ready guide, but it throws us on a knowledge of the heart of God. It is here that we found a chink in our learned Doctor's armour. However it may be with him, I do not know how I am to trust my own heart to echo the divine, without that union with God in Christ, which our religion promises to the believing penitent.

We have said that the saving action of Christ begins with mystical union, or incorporation, and also ends in it. What is this union, so far as it affects the believer's will? Does it consist simply in formal agreement? For example, the authorities of my College make rules, and perhaps the junior members of the College loyally observe them. There is formal agreement, then, between their wills and the will of the Governing Body. Yet the motives of the undergraduates in observing the rules, and the motives of the Governing Body in making them, though both, let us hope, laudable, may be widely different. But now a somewhat absurd situation arises. On a night of general merrymaking, the members of another college make a mock-serious incursion upon us. The Dean of the College, entering into the spirit of the occasion, calls on his young men to help him drive the marauders out. In such an action the Dean and those it is his normal duty to discipline are of one heart and mind; they are all boys together. This is something more than a formal identity of will. Yet it is still a poor parable of what we are after. No man can stand to another in the relation in which our Creator stands to us. It is his prerogative to make his creatures make themselves. For the most part they are utterly unaware of his doing so. His will does not penetrate into their wills, even supposing that they have wills. But a man brought into union with the divine life which beats in the pulses of Christ, hopes to be inspired; he hopes that his Creator's will may come through into his, and form it.

As soon as we speak of inspiration, we are suspected of claiming mysterious oracles and infallible guidances, somehow given to us from an untraceable source. The suspicion rests on the assumption that we locate inspiration in the mind. The assumption is incorrect. Though his mind is certainly cleared and assisted by inspiration, the inspiration of the common Christian is centred in his heart. Sheer mental inspirations are like miracles;

God may bestow them, we cannot count on them. They share with miracles another characteristic: it is hard to know when they are genuine and when they are not. It is otherwise with the inspiration of the heart. We can be reasonably sure of a good desire or attitude.

But if God inspires the heart rather than the intellect, it is not because mental inspirations are more precious, and he reserves them for the few and the spiritually advanced. On the contrary, the inspiration of the heart is infinitely more precious, for it brings us into union with the heart of God. I suppose it needs no words on our part to establish that a union with the heart of God is the first object of Christian prayer; and those who have any experience of true Christians will add that such union is also its most real fruit.

Inspiration is, to Christians, a matter of faith. In the degree and manner in which they commonly receive it, it is not anything that could be publicly proved; and it is difficult to conceive what tests could be devised which would supply the evidence. God convinces us, somewhat as our friends convince us, not by evidence but by quality. The profound seriousness with which Christians in fact take their inspiration is seen in their acknowledgement of the Holy Ghost as a Person of Godhead.

'Holy Ghost' means 'divine life bestowed'. The Holy Ghost is *Deus ut donum*, God in the guise of a gift. Admittedly the language of gift is mere metaphor, and so equally is the language of indwelling. The creature has no lap into which such a gift could be thrown, and offers no habitation where such a guest could lodge. The language of gift is, if anything, the more dangerous, for a gift is commonly something which the recipient is welcome to use. And so far from our using the Holy Ghost, it is our privilege to be at his disposal, as the host is at the disposal of an honoured guest. Still, there is something to be said on the other side. A guest comes and goes and does his pleasure; a gift is given away, and so expresses less inadequately the sheer generosity of God. The metaphors do what metaphors are good for; they show the moral colour of the divine action. If we wish to define what happens, we must say that the activity of God's will lives in the action of ours, so that we say 'The more it is God, the more it is I; and the more it is I, the more it is God'.

Anyone who has genuinely prayed will know what these words mean. Not that the prayers of Christians commonly achieve such a transparency to the will of God; we pray more by faith than by sight; yet we have our transparent times, and these offer the clue which our faith follows.

If we are simple Christians, yes; but suppose we have read the psychologists? Cannot psychology explain everything, without recourse to the supernatural? In exercises of prayer, they may tell us, we make the quick-moving top of our mind wait for the slow-moving depths. And so, for once in a way, our superficial good intentions are floated up on the rising waters of profound desire, and this is what we feel. We are united with ourselves.

Are the psychologists right? Of course they are right, anyhow in what they affirm. The Holy Ghost is not a feeling, or a finite psychological force. He could not conceivably feature in a psychological explanation along-side other forces or components of the human mind. He is God, and God is the universal underlying Cause, not any created or particular cause. He does not inject anything into us, called either charity or inspiration. He continues the creation of our being out of its existing materials, and these are earthly enough. In particular, he creates that union of surface desire with profound intention, which psychology describes.

But the crucial point has still to be mentioned. The sanctifying action of the Holy Ghost is no mere name for any unification of the self which may have the sort of effect we have roughly depicted. The self may be pulled together by any object, interest or pursuit which is capable of drawing our deep instinctive urges in the direction of a conscious purpose. The action of the Holy Ghost unites us about a centre which lies outside ourselves, in the heart of God.

Everything in a praying mind that could conceivably be amenable to psychological description is open to the psychologist. The divine impact mediated by these mental facts is not a psychological object at all. A psychological study may similarly be made in the image of your friend which you carry in your mind, and the pattern which your affections and ideas form round the focus of that image. But the question whether your friend is what you think him, or even whether he is a dream companion and has no existence, is not a psychological question; and neither is the question concerning the reality of the Holy Ghost. The comparison is valid, even though the relation is not the same; the Holy Ghost 'underlies' you, your friend confronts you. Neither is you, or any part of you; and that negative is all that is needed to give force to the analogy.

The topic of spiritual psychology, which I have

touched upon here, deserves a much fuller and certainly a more positive treatment than I can afford it. The last thing I should wish to do is suggest that the principal concern a theologian has with psychology is to point out its limitations. How to be sane, though saintly; how to minimize tensions, and avoid delusions; how, even, to pray so as to bring the whole man into the prayer; where to locate and how to draw off the springs of temptation—here are topics on which spiritual directors have accumulated lore, and psychological science can throw further light. I wish St. Symeon Stylites had had a psychologist to consult before he mounted his solitary pillar. Our present concern is to examine Christian beliefs, not to delve into spiritual phenomena. Only, if one says nothing about the phenomena, there is a danger of leaving the beliefs both unrelated to reality, and unshielded from attack.

However that may be, the next turn of the discussion will lift us abruptly back to the doctrinal plane. We have said something about the Holy Spirit in relation to the lives of Christians; our next task is to relate him to the person of Christ. I can remember how puzzling I once felt this relation to be; and remembering my own old difficulties, I can well imagine that what I have so far written may have puzzled my readers. It would seem to me very reasonable if their reactions were somewhat as follows. 'Here is the figure of a divine-human Christ, bringing the Godhead into human neighbourhood, and through kind but relentless proximity breaking down enmity by suffering, until our reconciliation is achieved by his death. What more can be needed for our perfection, than the continuing presence and impact of such a Christ? Well, but apparently there is more; yes, I can see that something more is possible. In the person of Christ, God acts through and as a man placed in the world beside me. But—yes—it is possible to conceive a still more intimate incursion of the divine. Perhaps the very ground of my being may be broken up, and the charity of God may spring in my heart. I see the amazing possibility; who is to deny that it lies within the power of God? Only, if this is possible, and actually available to religious faith, why is there, why ever was there any need for the intervention of Christ? The religion of the Spirit is all-sufficing. If the Creator can act on his creatures from the ground of the heart, and in the very springing-point of the will, why may not the Holy Ghost convert and inspire mankind, and so procure our salvation of his sole motion?'

The answer to such a question must be sought for in the nature of our freewill. God makes his creatures make themselves, and they must truly make themselves by their own principle of action. We are not to conceive that God throws such a responsibility on them by a special decree of his will, or that he might have ordained otherwise. It is rather that their action is their existence, and if they did not act of themselves, they would not exist in themselves—in fact, God would have failed after all to create them. Now we said that the Holy Ghost is not a gift for us to use as we like, but a power using us at his good pleasure. Nevertheless our freewill is his instrument, and he does not force it; he does not do with us anything that the set of our own purpose debars. His action is like the rising water of the tide, ready to fill every cranny that opens in the reef it engulfs, yet forcing no openings that are not offered.

He does, in some sense, wait for the action of sinful creatures. It could not be otherwise. So, then, if God wills to convert us, it cannot be from beneath the springing-point of our will. To say that we need conversion is to say that the channel is blocked. What, then, does he do? He forces upon us conditions in our creaturely environment which challenge our voluntary response, and, when the response is unworthy, shows it up for what it is. So Christ bears upon mankind, and his crucifixion shows us what we are. And it is by continued association with Christ that we are opened to the action of the Holy Ghost.

To the Christian mind the case of the Christian believer is the perfect or typical case. That is not to say that the Holy Ghost has no scope of action in any but Christian hearts. There is, as it were, a Christ-factor where there is not Christ; there are human examples, relationships, circumstances, demands external to the man, which bear upon him and elicit from him those responses in which the divine Spirit acts. He acts, of course, from the very start. No Christian wants to say, 'I respond to Christ and *then* the Holy Ghost supports me.' Conversion is the capture of a town, by the joint effort of an assault from without, and a fifth column within. Apart from the pressure from without, the fifth column would be held down. Apart from the action of the column, the assault would not breach the defences.

It is the testimony of Scripture that Jesus himself was full of the Holy Ghost. An inspiration which was primarily his spread to his disciples, in proportion as they came, by adoption, to partake in his Sonship. It looks strange at first sight that one in whom the divine life personally dwelt should require inspiration; and hasty students of the New Testament have concluded that it contains two incompatible pictures of Christ; the Son of God by inspiration, the Son of God in nature and in person. I call the conclusion hasty, because it fails to notice some of the most striking of the evidence; I mean that the texts which are highest in their doctrine of Christ's Sonship-by-nature are also most emphatic in their witness to his filial inspiration. I suppose it will be admitted that no New Testament writer holds a higher doctrine of Christ's divine person than St. John does. St. Thomas speaks for the evangelist, when he makes his profession of faith, 'My Lord and my God.' Yet nowhere is it so plain as in St. John's Gospel, that Christ's Sonship is a continual dependence on his Father's Spirit. He neither speaks, nor acts of himself; his Father in him is the doer of his works. He has all the glory in the world, because his Father's glory is his; he has no glory in himself, but only what his Father bestows.

If there is a contradiction between an inspired Christ and a divine Christ it is a contradiction St. John did not feel. If we feel it, let us put our difficulty to the Evangelist and see what he says. How (we ask him) could God the Son need the inspiration of his Father's Spirit? St. John looks at us in plain amazement. '*Need*,' he replies, 'what makes you say *need*?—as though he would be more perfect, if he did without the Spirit of God. As well ask why a man *needs* a mind; it would be far better, no doubt, to be an unthinking beast; but by an unlucky accident the beast called man is so complex in his animal organization, he has to be helped out by the gift of mentality. Do you think so? Of course not. To have mental powers and to use them is a glory and a blessing; but a greater glory and a greater blessing still is to be indwelt by the Father's Spirit. We creatures of God, and sons by adoption, have such a gift of the Spirit as our nature or our virtue allows; we are narrow vessels at the best, giving but little scope to the Spirit of God. But the being of the divine Son is the vessel which gives full scope to the Holy Ghost. He can and does receive all the Father has to bestow, and that is all that the Father himself is; he does not give him his Spirit by measure. What is this talk of *needing*? It is not even as though the Son had once been without the Spirit, and needed to receive him. It would be about as sensible to say that we creatures of God needed existence, until it pleased God to bestow it upon us. We were not there, to need existence or anything else, until God called us into being, and then we had it. If, to suppose the impossible, such creatures as we are could have existed of ourselves apart from God, we should not have been the richer for it, but infinitely the poorer; it is more blessed to be rooted in the Supreme Will, than to be (were that possible) in a godless, uncreated world. There never was a divine Son who needed the Spirit; there always was a Son fulfilled with the Spirit; whom the Father eternally begets, him he eternally indwells.'

Such is, I think, the answer of St. John. I know I have made him talk an idiom later than his own; I do not think I have misrepresented his faith. I made him quote by the way one sentence from his own book; the reader may find it if he likes.

I am now going to make an observation not about realities but about words. By orthodox definition the Holy Ghost is the Third Person of the Blessed Trinity. Why 'Person'? Many mystifying things have been said about the meaning this word is supposed to have carried at the time when the standard doctrinal definitions were made. In fact, there is no mystery at all. 'Person' then meant exactly what it means now—not in such rather special uses as 'John is really quite a person'— 'Do you think the person is to be found in the body or in the soul?' but in commonplace usages, such as 'We touched at Cherbourg and twenty persons came on board'—though I am afraid it has to be admitted that we now say 'people'. The beauty of 'person' was simply that 'persons' do not absolutely have to be human: if you were telling a story about a man, his guardian angel and his besetting demon, by what single term would you describe your three characters? If there was one thing rather than another that 'person' suggested, it was a character in a play or narrative. To say that there are three Persons of Godhead would have naturally suggested then just what it suggests now—that the mysterious life of the Godhead is to be thought of by us in the human parable of a story about three characters. If so, the suggestion was and is misleading. The revealed parable of the Godhead is a story about two characters, Father and Son. Only, we add, since the Father in this case is not a human father, but the first of all persons; and since the Son is not son to a man, but Son to his God; therefore the Father does not merely beget the Son, he also indwells him by his Spirit.

Why, then, you may well ask, was the Holy Ghost called 'Person' by orthodox definition? I can only reply, Because the Latins could not hit upon a better word. The Greeks who formulated the definition avoided the corresponding term and used a more abstract, non-committal one. What the Greeks said, and the Latins must be credited with trying to say, was simply this: The Spirit is the divine life, is God, God the self-bestowing or indwelling, God finding scope of action in the being or action of another; the first other in whom he finds such scope being the eternal Son, himself also God.

We will not look further into these mysteries. The Holy Ghost is God; yet the Trinity is not (in human terms) a society of three, but a society of two, inspiring and inspired. Only, whereas the Father and the Son belong to the human parable as well as to the divine fact, the inspiration does not; not, that is, inspiration in the required sense. Of course it may be that a son finds his parent what is called 'inspiring', but inspiring-ness in so washed-out a sense is merely misleading for our theological purpose. No, the inspiration is what is distinctive of the divine mystery, it shows where the human parable of Father and Son breaks down. Inspiration is the act of God alone. Fathers and sons are humdrum, even animal occurrences; inspirations are not.

But if inspiration is not a human fact, but purely divine, then how is it that this element in the pattern of the Trinity means anything to us at all? What is our clue? Our clue lies in the inspirations which, by the pure work of God, are given to men. We know the Spirit in the Trinity because we know him in our souls. If a man has no sense of what it is to be inspired, even in his prayer, we shall talk to him in vain about the Holy Ghost.

Not that the Holy Ghost is anything that we feel. For first, we cannot feel him, even when he signifies his action to us by the force and direction he gives to our aspiration; and second, the most part of his action is without any awareness in those he inspires. Where we recognize the signal action of the Spirit in the lives of saints, they may have been least aware of any such grace. They were (for example) wholly engrossed with the people who drew forth their charitable concern. But where there is the self-forgetting charity of saints, there, surely, is the Holy Ghost.

In talking of the Spirit we started on earth and soared away into heaven; and now here we are back on earth again, speaking of the inspirations God bestows. Before we took off, when we still had our heels on the ground, we were saying that association with Christ and inspiration belong together, the impact of Christ opening us to the Spirit of God, and the Spirit of God inspiring our response to Christ. Though we do not wish to say that either comes before the other, yet the way to seek the inspiration is to look towards Christ; and where is he? Our association is not with a dead but with a living saviour. The Son of God not only exists in his eternal being, he lives in our world, that is, in the body of mankind; though his place is in that vastly greater part of the human fellowship which has migrated out of the visible world by death; in his case, by death and resurrection. He remains on the human side of the great divide.

It is a sort of childishness we all commit, unless we consciously correct it, to work with a two-decker scheme of heaven and earth. That is our great divide: on earth the familiar presences of flesh and blood, in heaven the mysterious Trinity, the holy angels, and the souls of Aunt Betty and Cousin David, departed from us in faith. When we think or imagine in such a form, what are we doing? We go as far as the first fence we meet, the barrier which closes our earthly perspective, and there we stop. Everything that lies beyond we lump together, as though there were no further fences dividing the territory. But the great divide—incomparably wider than any other, since its width is infinite—is the gulf which separates the God-head from all and any created being. This is the Atlantic Ocean. The division between angels and men is only a parish boundary; that between men living and departed, a hedge between two fields. The Son of God is still on our side of the ocean, and in our parish, too, by his continued incarnation, or personal identity with the risen Jesus; only he is on the other side of the hedge from us. The company Christ has associated with himself is on both sides of the hedge; Christ is a man among men and we have fellowship with him by prayer and sacrament.

In certain early professions of faith, such as were made by candidates for baptism, acknowledgement of Holy Church was linked with acknowledgement of Holy Spirit, as though one were naming the soul and the body respectively of a mystical communion. Christ is the primary bearer of the Holy Ghost; when he extends the spiritual gift to others he extends his person through them. As all the limbs and other parts animated by your biological life-pattern are your body, so all those inspired with the Spirit are the body of Christ, 'and severally members thereof'.

Such a way of looking at things opens up the whole subject of the Church, and of the Sacraments, into which I do not propose to enter. I will limit myself to a single remark, more in correction of false impressions I may have made, than with any idea of opening

a new field. I fear I have over-individualized the posses-
sion of the Spirit. Does the endowment belong to the
individual, and not rather to the Church?

There is one very plain sense in which only the
individual can be inspired. Only the individual has a
personal life, only he exercises an act of will which
the Spirit may supernaturalize. Nevertheless the individual member need not be, and indeed is not, inspired
without regard to the whole body. It may well be that
we do not commonly receive inspiration, and certainly
have no right to ask it, for ourselves alone. The Holy
Ghost is the imparted love of God; it is love that he
inspires and love is both outgoing and corporative.

To go a point further, there may be, and are, inspirations given to individuals for action on behalf of
the body, or in so far as they share with the body,
incorporating themselves in it; say by receiving the
sacraments. Exactly to define how far the Spirit moulds
his action upon the form of the Church would be a
subject of the greatest difficulty. Let us simply say
that to hold the Church in any estimation is to believe
that he does so in some manner; and that no Christians
suppose him to be bound by the physical limits and
lineaments of the Church. The sacraments are covenanted
mercies; of uncovenanted mercies the number is infinite,
and the scope unknown.

# Heaven and Hell

'Oh, do stop talking about me marrying you!' says the hard-hearted girl. 'It's so mercenary of you. Can't you like me a bit as I am? Is there nothing in it for you except getting me?'—'Don't be so maddening,' says the young man. 'It's absolute heaven being with you; but it can't be the same thing going around with you an evening now and then. You can call it mercenary if you like, but it takes all the heaven out of it if it isn't going to lead to anything solid in the end. That's how men mostly feel, so what's the use of pretending?'

Perhaps this particular method of keeping young men on pins is no longer much in fashion, but even last year's girl will do for this year's parable. A parable of what? Surely the answer is obvious. 'Oh, do stop talking about heaven!' says the spiritual-minded girl. 'It's so mercenary. Don't you have to say it's a privilege to serve God in this life? Is there nothing in it for you unless you are to be paid for it? and how paid? By having your precious self preserved when the world has no more use for your precious services. If you like, I'll say it's an even bet whether there's a life after this, or not. But what can you do about it? Not a thing, except live decently now; and you'd want to do that in any case. Why bother about the hereafter? Why not just leave it to God?'

'Don't be so maddening,' answers the young man.

'My precious self, indeed! What about other people's precious selves? I suppose you'll allow me to care for other people, even if you object to my caring for you. Do you think it makes no difference my believing that the people I care for are going to go on, and arrive somewhere? Otherwise it all seems such a farce; the whole human product forced forward with all this trouble, only to leak away out of the pipe of history and vanish in the sand.'

'Nonsense!' says the girl. 'You think you care about the others, you are really worried about yourself. It's that sick feeling inside, when you think of dying, that bothers you.'

'Of course it bothers me,' says he, 'to have a protest against death thumping inside my ribs. That's how I know how other people feel about it. Otherwise I wouldn't know. I can't experience their emotions from the inside, can I? If my death isn't an outrage, why should anyone's be?'

'Ah, *Thou wast not born for death, immortal bird*,' said Keats to the nightingale, but he knew he was lying. The early worm gets the immortal bird, so why not the immortal bard? Nature cries out against death, right enough, but that's natural death; and you've got to go through with that, in any case. There are plenty of things nature cries out against, and they happen, just the same: senility, for example.'

'Look,' says the young man, 'you've got me on to a bad wicket by starting up this stuff about the sick feeling inside. That's just animal, and animals aren't immortal, whatever the dog-lovers say. Or—well, no, the feeling's not merely animal; it involves imagining the future in a way animals presumably don't. All the same, I wouldn't want to claim that every animal able to imagine its future becomes a candidate for immortality.'

'Oh, you wouldn't?' says the girl. 'Then what *would* you want to claim?'

Her friend looks puzzled, and frowns for a minute. 'It's no use me pretending to have thought of this one myself,' he says at last, 'but they say we are made in the image of God, and it's an amazing thing, when you look at it, this power we have of thinking ourselves out of our own skins, and taking a God's-eye view. And what I say is, creatures that can get outside their skins may be candidates for a life outside their skins, when, as the burial service says, worms destroy this body.'

'Candidates,' says the girl, 'candidates if you like; but not all candidates get elected.'

'Well, it depends on the Electorate,' says the youth, 'which happens in this instance to be dependable.'

'I know,' says she, 'and it's easy to say that if God wants us, he'll keep us; and if he didn't want us, why did he reveal himself to us? The weak spot in the argument is skated over, as usual. What needs showing is that God *can* make men immortal.'

'What do you mean?' says he. 'If God is God, he can do all things.'

'All things,' she says, 'but not any nothings; a square circle is a nothing and you won't find him making many of those. Perhaps a human personality parted from its body is a nothing too, a meaningless idea. God can make me—right, for so he has, through the natural process. And if I die tomorrow, he can make another girl as like me as two peas—right, I suppose he can. But can he make her be personally the same girl as me?

We just don't know enough to say whether he can, or not.'

'No, we don't,' her friend admits, 'and how could we? We don't know by what sort of joint the new immortal life would fit on to the old decaying one; for we don't know what the new life is going to be like itself, for a start. But anyhow, we can't prove the negative; we can't show that God is unable to let us carry on after death somewhere else if he likes, and on a different level altogether.'

' "Can't prove the negative" is a long way from "Should believe the positive",' says the girl. 'You can't prove there aren't pink kangaroos on Mars.'

The young man, not seeing his way out of the argument, tries another line. 'We're straying from the point,' he says. 'I've let you get away with your original and really beastly remark about my being mercenary for wanting heaven. Wanting heaven is like wanting you; if I didn't hope you'd have me in the end, getting to know you wouldn't be—well, wouldn't be what it is. Of course I know I may not get you, you may be a step on the way to someone else.' (The girl made him a mock bow.) 'But God can't be on the road to some other God, for there isn't any other God. And the religion we have in this world is a pathetic sort of bit, a beginning without any ending, if we aren't to get to God at last, and have eternity to know him. Who gets to grips with God in this life, I'd like to know, or for that matter, gets to grips with himself? And it isn't only idle skunks like me who say so; these incredible mystics and saints and people, the more they do get a grip, the more they see how far off they are. Mercenary, my foot! It's mercenary to want payment for a job. I never heard it was mercenary to want to make a job of the job. But that's a rotten way of talking, too; you don't say *Make a job of* a love or a friendship. We want to get right into it, though, and come to terms with the person; and if the person is God . . .'

The speaker felt himself unequal to the subject, and even the lady failed to come up with a bright remark. Suddenly he started again. 'You and your blue kangaroos,' he said.

'Pink kangaroos,' she corrected. 'On Mars. Nonexistence of, indemonstrable. Existence of, improbable.'

'Very well,' he said, 'and why improbable?'

'I'll tell you why,' said she. 'First, kangaroos don't come pink; second, there's nothing known about Mars that's likely to strike them pink, or to favour the production of kangaroos, whether pink or otherwise. The order of nature, as far as we know it, isn't set towards throwing pink kangaroos, and least of all on Mars.'

'Correct,' says the man, 'but how does it apply? The order of nature isn't set towards throwing immortalized men, how could it be? Immortalized man is beyond nature, anyhow. If people believe in immortalized man, what do they think is set towards throwing him? Not the natural process, obviously. Do we have to say, The supernatural process? and what on earth should we mean by it?'

'You don't seem much good at finishing your own arguments,' says the girl. 'I'd have thought that according to your story, God's dealing with mankind in their religion is set in the direction of immortalizing them. Your argument is, the whole process points that way.'

'There now!' says the other. 'A woman must have

the last word. Let's leave it at that—and you'll have
had it—on my side of the argument.'

'Of course I'm on your side,' says the girl. 'I only
wanted you to stop being so mercenary.'

'Mercenary!' says he—and since the argument looks
like coming round again in a circle, we had better
leave the pair of them to it; we shall get on faster by
ourselves. We will begin by listing a few principles
which emerged in the course of the wrangle.

1. To hope for heaven has nothing particularly selfish
   about it. No one ever thought he could keep heaven
   to himself.
2. Heaven is not a cash payment for walking with God;
   it's where the road goes.
3. Heaven isn't an optional extra; our belief is nonsense
   without it.
4. Our reason for believing it isn't that nature points to
   it, but that it leads us to itself.

I should like to develop the last point a bit. Heaven
is nothing that created nature produces; it is a new
creation. Two consequences follow from this. The first
is, that we have no interest in trying to isolate a piece
of us called soul, which tends to outlive the body's
collapse. Our immortality is the new gift of God, not
the survival of our old nature, whether in whole or in
part. It was pagan Greeks who talked about immortal
soul, and with reason; for (to put it shortly) they thought
the human spirit was a piece of godhead, able to
guarantee immortal being to itself. The religion of the
Bible teaches no such doctrine. God alone can give us
a future. It is better, then, to talk about the resurrection
of man than about the immortality of soul. Belief in
resurrection is belief not in ourselves, but in God

who raises us. It is in fact the acid test, whether we believe in God or not. A God who raises the dead is a real power; he is not just a fanciful name for the order of nature, whether physical or moral. A God so identified with the natural order that he adds nothing to it is difficult to distinguish from the world he rules, or from the laws which govern it.

Old Indian thought evaded the issue by making the cycle of the soul's rebirths a part of nature, like the seasons and the tides. And as the lazy mind need not distinguish the God of the tides from the tides, neither need it distinguish the cycles of rebirth from the God of the cycles. But when we realize that man's person, the living image of God, is bound to be sucked down in the whirlpool of decay, unless God rescues it; then faith in God begins to mean something. It alters the whole picture.

Now to take the second consequence. If the heavenly state is not something nature produces, but something God bestows, our ideas of heaven are bound to be ideas of a relation to God. Not that the heavenly state can simply consist of a relation to God; the citizens of heaven must have some way of being which is proper to them, some nature which God gives them; only we do not happen to know what it is. The other day I had occasion to look at a sermon of St. Augustine's, which speculates on the resurrection-body. It will not, the saint thinks, be made in the stuff of flesh and blood. These baser substances will transmute to something rich and strange, the substance of glory. Still, the lineaments will remain. But what of the organs for which we have no further use, the digestive and such like? Shall we have them, or not? The saint sees himself poised on the brink of absurdity, and pulls back his foot. Nature, he says, makes all the parts to serve a double purpose, use and beauty; beauty will endure, when use is at an end. Even those parts now thought uncomely are only so thought because we have such nasty minds. If we feel shy of stripping to the eye of heaven, we can be assured that our personal deformities will have been cleared up, but not in such a way as to impair our individualities.

What is perhaps even more curious than St. Augustine's speculation is Harvey's respect for it. Harvey, that great pioneer of medical science, argues from St. Augustine in his anatomy lectures, that the principle of beauty is more dominant in the shaping of the body than the principle of function. For Nature has supreme regard to the ultimate end; and function is temporal, beauty eternal. I do not know whether it was such reasoning as this that led him to discover the circulation of the blood.

There is nothing the matter with St. Augustine's speculation, so long as he is content to put it in the form of a question. Our future self must bear some relation to our present self and it is a fair enough enquiry, what the relation will be. The angels know the answer, we do not; and it is evident that invention of the kind St. Augustine develops is not what gives a positive content to our notion of the heavenly state. Nor, of course, the white raiment, the psalteries and the palms. Anyone who takes these things as literal realities, distinguishing life on Mount Zion from life on Hampstead Hill, must anticipate an everlasting boredom. Such symbols find their proper place in the suggestion of a worship which truly satisfies.

It is silly to say, 'How marvellous to be in heaven! Our shirts will be whiter than the latest detergent can wash them, and we shall have no need to switch on the electric light.' It is not silly to say, 'Every now and then, perhaps, I manage to be at the disposal of God's will. How marvellous to be in heaven! I shall live in it all the time.' Nor is it silly to say, 'From time to time I think I catch a glimpse of what God is doing. How marvellous to be in heaven! I shall see his purposes in everything, as clearly as I read my friends' feelings on their faces.' Nor is it silly to say, 'Every now and then I see a bit of what God has put into the people round me. How marvellous to be in heaven! I shall see it all.' Nor is it silly to say, 'I acknowledge Christ by faith, and bless him in words for being very God and very man. How marvellous to be in heaven! I shall be familiar with the man in whom the Godhead is.'

If you consider the marvels I have mentioned, you will notice three things that are true of them all. First, they are joys of which we have a foretaste in this life; and so we know what we are talking about when we mention them. Second, they are joys which arise from a more perfect relation with realities—with God and with the children of God. Third, they are joys which might be actualized (for anything we know) under a variety of conditions, or states of being. Our faith in heaven is a confidence in the pattern of perfect relations; as for the state of being, we can leave it to God.

It is often said that heaven is the presence of God. There is nothing wrong with the formula, so long as it is taken to mean that the presence of God is what makes heaven heavenly. It is nonsense if it means that the presence of God defines a region or even a condition

in which the blessed dead find themselves. You can't
enter the presence of God by exchanging life for death
as you might enter the presence of a monarch by leaving
the anteroom for the throne-room; or as though this
world were a shuttered house, and to get out of it were
to be in an open air where God is.

> There's a great deal to be said
> For being dead,

but there isn't all that to be said for it. Let us recall
a few basic truths of theology.

First, there is no God-space or God-state, in which
God is and other things can lodge. God is his own
world of being; he fills it and nothing can share it.
Second, nothing else exists unless God creates it in its
own world and on its own level, not in his world nor
on his level. So if heaven exists, it exists by God's
creation; he creates or upholds the real beings of whom
heaven is made up, and he ordains the pattern of their
mutual relations. Third, God is everywhere by his
activity and his will; nothing would anywhere exist
if he were not with it, willing and upholding it. Fourth,
if God is anywhere more than elsewhere, it is because
he works there more richly and more revealingly. He
is more present in men than in beasts, in Christians
than in pagans, in saints than in Laodiceans; it is but
a further step to add, more in heaven than on earth.

Heaven, then, is a created sphere where God bestows
his presence by his action, especially his action through
heart and mind. And where is heaven? When I was a lad
it was still supposed to be an insoluble problem. If
heaven is completely non-spatial, then (we used to say)
the heavenly life must be a featureless sea of feeling,

a shapeless ecstasy; or anyhow, nothing you could fairly call the resurrection-state of man. Whereas if heaven has any form of spatial dimension, then it falls somewhere in the field of space; a telescope might record it, an astronaut might reach it. And so heaven is pulled back into the perishable universe.

A pretty puzzle, and I was amazed to hear it solemnly restated the other day by a professor of philosophy; for I had supposed that Einstein had shown it up once for all as a piece of nonsense. According to his unanswerable reasoning, space is not an infinite pre-existent field or area in which bits of matter float about. Space is a web of interactions between material energies which form a system by thus interacting. Unless the beings or energies of which heaven is composed are of a sort to interact physically with the energies in our physical world, heaven can be as dimensional as it likes, without ever getting pulled into our spatial field, or having any possible contact with us of any physical kind. There may well be contacts which are not physical at all between earthly minds and heavenly minds, but that's another story. How I wish we could explain the Einsteinian theory to St. Augustine! Obviously his heaven is dimensional; but the stuff of glory which composes its constituents is surely not apt to interact with sticks and stones, with flesh and blood.

Think what we may of heavenly dimensions, heaven is a sphere of created being, where God bestows his presence. And this he does at least in three ways: by a more visible providence, making the whole order of things the evident expression of an infinite goodness; by a more abundant grace, making the minds of his people transparent to his thought and their hearts to his love; by an incarnate presence with them in the glorified man, Jesus Christ.

Christ in glory is the heart of heaven, and it is difficult to see how those Christians who leave the life to come an open question can be Christians at all. If Christ is not now in glory, then this is a Christless world and God is a Christless God and we are Christless men. Those who say heaven is nothing to us now but an optional hope, may say the same of Christ; unless, that is, they have received a revelation not imparted to the rest of us, making heaven to be a place for one glorified man, and for no more.

Nothing is plainer in the faith of the New Testament than the ties attaching Christians to a living Christ. Because he is beyond the death we still have to face, our union with him is union with an achieved immortality. By dying, Christ not only made a supremely generous sacrifice, both overcoming enmity, and reconciling sinners to God; he also took the decisive step into that better state of being which lies beyond death. To grow up was good, to die was better; better, if only one could die right. Sinners die into death, but Christ, strong in the power of God, dies into better life. By communion with him, even in this present world, we plant a foot on the risen and spiritual state. Being incorporate with Christ, we are not only incorporate with the Son of God, we are incorporate with a man who has reached the goal of creaturely existence. Christ the infant was a less visible expression of divine sonship than Christ the man; and Christ the man of flesh and blood a less expression than Christ transfigured.

This annexing of an earthly fellowship to the heavenly state was begun when Christ, risen from death to glory,

HEAVEN AND HELL

visited his surviving friends. Nothing like it ever has happened, or can happen—that the heart of heavenly being should visit earth, to leave on earthly senses the stamp of heavenly substance. No thoughtful Christian can allow the Resurrection to be placed in one category with any other class of events, any more than he can allow God to be placed in one category with any class of beings.

It is our business to state the Christian belief, as well as to examine the grounds for it. In stating what it is, a Christian writer can scarcely help becoming somewhat exalted, especially if he dips his pen in St. Paul's inkpot, as we have just been doing. It may have a sobering effect, if we turn to the other branch of our duty and ask a critical question. Why should anyone believe in the life to come?

The old-fashioned answer was, 'Because God has promised it.' If you asked how and where they turned you up Bible texts. God had written the book, God could not lie. It is difficult for us to recapture so submissive an attitude to the written word. I would like to keep the formula, nevertheless: God has promised it, even though the fact is not sufficiently shown by citing chapter and verse. I should want to say that God's promise is a rope of several strands. If we untwist the rope, and take the strands separately, then very likely no one of them seems sufficient to take the weight. But they belong together, and there is no reason why they should not be allowed the mutual support they naturally offer one another. They are not five promises, but one.

First there is the promise which lies in the very nature of man. Since the promise is God's promise, it depends on man's being the creature of God; it is not a promise atheists could read. But allowing that the creator has control over his works, we ask what he means by bringing up a creature capable of immortal hope; capable besides of drawing on the source of everlasting renewal by a personal and voluntary attachment to his creator. Does not the Maker show his hand? Is there not an implicit promise of immortalization in the nature of such a creature as this?

The weakness of the promise lies in its inarticulate character; it lies buried in the facts, we have to spell it out by our own reasoning effort, and we are too familiar with the suspicion that a counter reason can be found to every reason. But though this strand would not bear the weight alone, it contributes greatly to the strength of the cord. The more striking and positive promises might appear irrational and isolated by themselves. It is otherwise if we can see them to lie in the line of a purpose which our very creation suggests.

The second strand we may take to be the teaching of Christ. It is not merely that so divine a teacher made his own a hope of future life which had begun to dawn in Israel. It is that he wagered his existence on it; that he accepted an early and a violent death as the gate of a kingdom in which he was appointed to rule the people of God.

The third strand is the evidence for the fulfilment of his hope; that is, of the resurrection. His body was not found, his friends could pay it no cult, his enemies could not use it in disproof of the gospel. And by visitations of his presence which they could not disbelieve, he convinced his disciples of a miracle which laid the cornerstone of heaven.

The fourth strand is the possibility which Christians find of relation to a living Christ.

The fifth is the orientation of such religious life as God's grace gives us, or as our co-operation allows. If it is real to us, how can the end be unreal to which it tends, and from which it derives its meaning?

It would be possible to distinguish further strands in the rope of promise, but at least the five we have named are vital; vital not only to the strength of the whole cord, but also to one another. The Gospel-facts would not convince, if they were not real in our present experience. Present experience would not convince us even when overlaid upon the Gospel facts, if it found no foundation in the nature of man as a created being.

I have contented myself with a bare enumeration of my five strands, because the matter of them has either been discussed already, or is too familiar to require discussion. I will, however, take up the second strand for further comment, the strand which lay in the teaching of Christ. It must be immediately obvious that an appeal to Christ's authority is without force for those who see nothing divine in his doctrine. But those who take a more positive attitude may still distinguish one part of his teaching from another; certain elements contain the heart of the matter, others are more in the nature of period trappings. On which side, they may ask, do we place the sayings about immortal hope? Was not Christ's essential message a proclamation of the kingdom of God, a declaration of its ethic or its spirit, and an embodiment of it in a fellowship transcending national boundaries? Like other Jewish teachers of the day, he taught a life to come;

but we have to observe that he connected it with historical predictions, and that these were not visibly fulfilled.

What I have to say is that such a dividing up of Christ's teaching cannot be fairly maintained. His whole mission stands or falls with the proclamation of a world to come. Say if you like that he came to open up the kingdom of God. But how was the Father's will to be made effectively sovereign and his creatures so united with their Maker as to possess their true happiness? Did Christ ever see such a consummation as a present possibility? No. The offer of the kingdom was made in the present; its achievement was promised for a future transformed by some divine mysterious change. It will scarcely surprise us that Christ spoke of the road into that future under the time-honoured symbols of Jewish prophecy, up to the moment when he realized through his own existence the way of death and resurrection. The disciples still had to learn through their existence what the path for them would be. Jerusalem fell, the age did not end. The road runs on, but none who walk it have far to go before they meet their saviour and their judge. History looks like an unbroken chain; for any human soul the partition between life and death is thin as paper.

Christians profess a credal belief in God and resurrection to eternal life. They do not profess such belief in the devil or in everlasting torment. The doctrine of hell has certainly found a place in authoritative statements of Christian teaching; it has never formed part of a creed properly so called (the Athanasian creed is not a creed, whatever it may be). Try the experiment of tacking on to the Apostles Creed or the Nicene 'and in one devil, tempter and enemy of souls; and in damnation to hell everlasting.' Now say the whole creed and see what it feels like. I can promise you it will feel pretty queer; and the queerness will be due to a swapping of horses in midstream; you jump from one act of belief to a different sort of act, when you pass from the God-and-heaven clauses to the devil-and-hell clauses. The belief which is expressed by credal profession is a laying hold on the objects of belief; or still more, perhaps, a laying of ourselves open to be laid hold of by them. But there is no question of our laying ourselves out to be laid hold of by hell or by Satan. That cannot be the object of the exercise. Christians may believe there is a hell. They do not believe in hell as they believe in heaven. For they do not put their faith in it.

The tough stomach of old-fashioned piety was able to digest a two-side meditation, setting hellish pains against heavenly joys. It is notorious, for example, what a place the founder of the Jesuits gave to that meditation in his spiritual exercises. But even if you are prepared to make his meditation in the approved form, you cannot fail to see how differently the pains and the joys function in the spiritual process. Hell is simply something to be shuddered from, not anything that gives shape to your Christian existence. Heaven shows the meaning of everything; hell shows the meaning of nothing, except by contrast, as dark shows the quality of light. The path St. Ignatius's disciple has to tread is mapped by the heaven to which it leads, not by the hell it shuns.

Here is another mental experiment for you. Try rewriting Bunyan's Pilgrim along the following lines. The man Christian is warned to flee from the City of

Destruction before it suffers the fate of Sodom and
Gomorrah. He gets out into the country in the nick of
time and wonders which way to run. He is shown no
guiding light, no royal road to the city of God. He
simply observes that the whole area is scarred with
moving craters and earthquake fissures, exhaling brim-
stone and disclosing grisly figures armed with outsize
toasting-forks. 'All these cracks and holes,' he tells
himself, 'lead straight to hell. I must keep dodging
them; I must follow the edges of firm ground, whether
they lead anywhere or nowhere. I must keep it up as
long as I live.'

Running from hell never was a programme. The
programme is to travel towards heaven. The meditation
on hell could at the most remind us how bad a thing
it is to fall down on our assignment. It may still be
that hellish nightmares may poison our religion, and
make heaven more an escape from pain than a fruition
of God. But that would be a disease of the imagination,
a psychological infirmity. It was not St. Ignatius's
intention. He hoped that heaven would capture our
hearts, and draw the whole force of our will towards
itself.

But you are probably not interested in St. Ignatius
or his exercises. You want to know whether Christians
are to believe everlasting torments, or not. Very well;
but I fear we must split the question up a bit.

The first point to be considered is the abstract
necessity of retributive justice. Emmanuel Kant thought
that if the world was to end tomorrow, we should still
hang a murderer today, for the sheer beauty of it.
Do you think so? I suspect that you do not. In an
imperfect world, it is necessary to enforce law by

threatening penalties. Some fool calls the bluff, and
then he is for it. We should like to let him off; but if
we do, the law will lose its force, and that will be a
worse thing for the community than the punishment
of an unsatisfactory citizen. The punishment is sad,
sordid and seldom good for the victim. It has an obvious
social utility; it corresponds to no high metaphysical
necessity that guilt should pay the price.

Hanging may be useful to a State. How can it serve
the purposes of God? Can he need the sanction of a
gallows, a gallows on which offenders wriggle for ever
and never lose consciousness of their condition? In
whose eyes is such a demonstration required, to save
the criminal law of the universe from falling into
contempt? The blessed do not need it, the damned
cannot profit by it, while we (who are under probation)
cannot witness it.

There seem to be only two credible reasons for
consigning souls to flame; either for remedial discipline,
or for extirpation. The idea of remedial discipline can
be readily understood. But we have freewill. Perhaps
no remedial sufferings, no persuasions of divine love,
will reconcile the rebel. Then what? He cannot be
found a place in everlasting bliss. But may not he be
dropped out of existence?

I have asked a number of questions without answering
them, and now I shall lay down positions without
proving them. I say, then, that the teaching of Christ,
the nature of our freewill, and the way God deals
with us all point in one direction: the loss of heaven
is a real danger. Second, I observe that Christ teaches
one thing with particular insistence. Men whose moral
misery is disguised from them by comfort, pride or

success, will find themselves after death a prey to that flame which can surely be nothing but the scorching truth. Third, I see that Christ speaks of the flame as everlasting, as a torment which does not lose its force, or die down. The sinner will vainly wait for it to exhaust itself, or hope to escape from it on to the further side. But I do not see that I am forbidden to ask, what then? Cannot everlasting Mercy save from everlasting fire, or let the irreconcilable perish in it?

The fate of ultimate impenitence is a mystery into which I am reluctant to look. If it overtakes any, I pray they may be few. But looking to myself, and the hopes a Christian dares to entertain, I find conscience and moral reason join forces with Catholic teaching, and forbid me to claim exemption from the burning of that flame. If Dives needed to be stripped, and to suffer the truth of his condition, do not we also? Perhaps, before we suffer it, we may be assured of mercy; perhaps the sight of mercy will make the torment, when we see what a God we have, and how we have served him; what wounds we have inflicted on the souls of our fellows by our egotism and neglect.

Purgatory was rejected by our Reformers, as undermining the sufficiency of Christ's atonement; for it was taken to be the serving of a sentence by which the guilt of Christians was in some way worked off. Such an objection has no force against the teaching, that we have a pain to pass through, in being reconciled to truth and love. And we may as well call this pain purgatorial, having no other name to call it. It seems strange, indeed, that so practical and pressing a truth as that of purgatory should be dismissed, while so remote and impractical a doctrine as the absolute everlastingness of hell should be insisted on. Nor is it that ultimate fire is scriptural, while remedial fire is not. Remedial fire was taught plainly enough by St. Paul to his Corinthians.

In conclusion I ought, perhaps, to touch upon a topic which is no very direct part of Christian belief, but which is likely to affect our sense of its reasonableness. What is the relation between salvation hereafter and Christian discipleship now? We cannot suppose that heaven is for Christians only, or that their position in it will be one of privilege. If, on the other hand, the Christian road is not the beaten track to heaven, we make the whole Christian effort an irrelevance, almost a farce. Besides, the mystery of our redemption, the supreme object of our faith, is stultified, if men can be reconciled to God otherwise than through Jesus Christ.

It used to be dramatically taught that between the Friday afternoon when he died and the dawn of Sunday when he rose, Christ's soul or spirit was among the dead, and that being there he did not lose his time. He preached the Gospel to the departed, and those who would have acknowledged him, had he lived in their days, acknowledged him there and then; for they were disembodied spirits, and in their action quick as thought. So Christ returned from the realms of death not solitary as he went, but leading Adam and Eve by the hand, a great train of their descendants following. He placed them in the Paradise of God, resumed his body, and visited his disciples. Christ's raid upon the world of ghosts was called 'the harrowing of hell'.

The mythical colouring of the scene will scarcely commend it to our belief, but the principles it embodies are rational enough. Those who died before Christ must be saved through Christ. Perhaps we would not wish to house them so discouragingly while they wait for Christ to come; but if we go so far as to place them already in heaven, we shall be struck by the surprising thought that it was a heaven without Christ, and therefore without the visible and incarnate presence of God. Can such a Christless state be heaven? Not if by heaven we mean that union with God, which is man's full beatitude. So we must call their happy limbo by some other name.

But if it could be conceived that a Christ dead and not yet risen might reconcile and receive those who, living before his time, had never known him, how far more readily may it be supposed that those who have died since without real opportunity to get a saving knowledge of him are reconciled by Christ in glory! The parable of sheep and goats shows Christ assembling all nations, and receiving into bliss those who, in succouring the wretched, had no knowledge that they were ministering to Christ.

If it be asked what the Church is for, supposing men can be saved as well without a knowledge of Christ in this life, various answers can be given. The first and most obvious is that the mercy of God desires to redeem as many souls as may be redeemed in this present existence; and by means of the Church to make the force of Christ felt even where he is not adored. The second answer is that the divine society must really and directly be built upon earth out of earthly materials. If it exists, it can welcome and assimilate multitudes from outside; otherwise there would be no heaven into which they might go; for heaven consists essentially of its citizens, not of jasper bulwarks, or pavements of transparent gold. We said just now that a heaven of souls without Christ would not be heaven; could we not say the same about a heaven of Christ without souls? Christ is not only God in man, he is God in mankind; God in one man isolated from all others would not even be God in man, for a man in isolation is not a human possibility. Christ's incarnation would have been nothing, but for his relation to his family, his disciples, and his nation; his continued incarnation after he rose would have been nothing but for his continuing relation with those he left on earth. Presently they joined him, one by one, in glory; and so that mystical body was built up, the nucleus of heaven, and the instrument of universal redemption. If those who know Christ in this life begin to complain, because multitudes who do not will one day be made equal with them, we know what Christ thinks of their attitude; it was one of his themes when he walked in Galilee, and taught his companions by his parables.